Some Men Are Our Heroes

The House of Prisca and Aquila

Our mission at the House of Prisca and Aquila is to produce quality books that expound accurately the word of God to empower women and men to minister together in a multicultural church. Our writers have a positive view of the Bible as God's revelation that affects both thoughts and words, so it is plenary, historically accurate, and consistent in itself; fully reliable; and authoritative as God's revelation. Because God is true, God's revelation is true, inclusive to men and women and speaking to a multicultural church, wherein all the diversity of the church is represented within the parameters of egalitarianism and inerrancy.

The word of God is what we are expounding, thereby empowering women and men to minister together in all levels of the church and home. The reason we say women and men together is because that is the model of Prisca and Aquila, ministering together to another member of the church—Apollos: "Having heard Apollos, Priscilla and Aquila took him aside and more accurately expounded to him the Way of God" (Acts 18:26). True exposition, like true religion, is by no means boring—it is fascinating. Books that reveal and expound God's true nature "burn within us" as they elucidate the Scripture and apply it to our lives.

This was the experience of the disciples who heard Jesus on the road to Emmaus: "Were not our hearts burning while Jesus was talking to us on the road, while he was opening the scriptures to us?" (Luke 24:32). We are hoping to create the classics of tomorrow: significant and accessible trade and academic books that "burn within us."

Our "house" is like the home to which Prisca and Aquila no doubt brought Apollos as they took him aside. It is like the home in Emmaus where Jesus stopped to break bread and reveal his presence. It is like the house built on the rock of obedience to Jesus (Matt 7:24). Our "house," as a euphemism for our publishing team, is a home where truth is shared and Jesus' Spirit breaks bread with us, nourishing all of us with his bounty of truth.

We are delighted to work together with Wipf and Stock in this series and welcome submissions on a wide variety of topics from an egalitarian inerrantist global perspective. The House of Prisca and Aquila is also a ministry center affiliated with the International Council of Community Churches.

For more information, contact housepriscaaquila@comcast.net.

Some Men Are Our Heroes

Stories by Women about the Men Who Have Greatly Influenced Their Lives

Edited by
KeumJu Jewel Hyun
Cynthia Davis Lathrop

Foreword by Alice P. Mathews

Preface by William David Spencer

WIPF & STOCK · Eugene, Oregon

SOME MEN ARE OUR HEROES
Stories by Women about the Men Who Have Greatly Influenced Their Lives

Wipf & Stock
An Imprint of Wipf and Stock Publishers
199 W. 8th Ave., Suite 3
Eugene, OR 97401
www.wipfandstock.com

ISBN 13: 978-1-60608-628-5

Manufactured in the U.S.A.

To all men who emulate Jesus' attitude toward women

Contents

Foreword by Alice P. Mathews ix
Preface by William David Spencer xiii
Acknowledgments xvii

1   Men of Excellence and Women of Endurance Bring Honor to God 1
    KeumJu Jewel Hyun

2   Special Men in the Life of a Congolese Professor 9
    Médine Moussounga Keener

3   Men Who Have Greatly Influenced My Life 26
    Judy W. Mbugua

4   Under the Mango Tree: A Missionary's Story 36
    Nancy Hudson

5   Who I Am: A Racing Car Driver Becomes a Globetrotting Professor 45
    Gwendolyn Joy Dewey

6   A Tribute to Those Who Helped Me Find My True Calling 59
    Elke Werner

7   Reflecting God's Image: A Father's Significance 68
    Cynthia Davis Lathrop

8   On Rising Up Above the Refugee Tent 76
    KeumJu Jewel Hyun

9   How a Man Can Help His Wife Become the Person God Intended 89
    Aída Besançon Spencer

10 Conclusion 100
    KeumJu Jewel Hyun and Cynthia Davis Lathrop

Afterword by John P. Lathrop 103
Contributors 106
Appendix by William David Spencer 110
Bibliography 113

Foreword

IN EARLIER TIMES, IT was called "the battle of the sexes." In more recent times, it is referred to as "the gender wars." "It," of course, is the relationship of men and women, which throughout history has often been more adversarial than collaborative. Various cultures set up such different expectations for men and for women that readers nod in agreement when reading books like John Gray's *Men Are from Mars, Women Are from Venus*. But under the misunderstandings about one another lie differences, not just in values, but in opportunity. For example, until the latter part of the nineteenth century, in North America women were barred from higher education and entrance in various professions. Even now, in the twenty-first century, in the workplace with professional training, they frequently earn less than their male peers doing the same jobs.

But the battle of the sexes has not focused only on differences in material opportunities in life. It has permeated the value, or lack of value, that men have placed on women or women have placed on men. An early second-wave feminist, Gloria Steinem, captured this in her statement that "a woman needs a man like a fish needs a bicycle." On the other hand, men have often limited their "need" for a woman to the need for sex or for a housekeeper.

None of this disparagement of the opposite sex was part of God's plan in creating humanity. In Genesis 1, we learn that God created both male and female in the divine image, and he gave to both of them the same double assignment: to have children together and to subdue the earth together (Gen 1:26–28). They were to work together in shared parenting and in providing for the children God gave them. A further hint of this togetherness comes in Genesis 2: The one thing in God's perfect creation that was not good was that the man should be alone and do his work alone (2:17). Because that was "not good," God gave him a companion who was his vis-á-vis (Hebrew *ezer knegdo*), someone like himself to work alongside him. Then, at the end of Genesis 2, God cemented this relationship (2:24) by asserting that the man would leave his father and mother and cleave to his wife, and the two would be one flesh.[1]

So there we have it: God's intention for the way men and women live and work together. But the story doesn't end in Genesis 2. Chapter 3 opens with a slithering serpent, a piece of forbidden fruit, and God's intended oneness for the man and woman shattered by sin followed by blaming and recrimination. The battle of the sexes had begun. And in many places and in many forms, it continues to this day.

It is a wonder, a joy, and a delight when we see individual men showing great respect for the women in their lives. And we are pleased when those women understand the gift such men are giving them through that respect and encouragement. In compiling this book, KeumJu Jewel Hyun and Cynthia Lathrop have reached around the world to bring us women's stories of the men who not only respected them, but who also encouraged them and opened doors of opportunity for them. These are men who reflect the intentions of their Creator, God, when he made humanity as male and female in the divine image.

In some cases, these men are decidedly countercultural in their encouragement of their daughters, their wives, or women in their spiritual care. In every case, these men reflect God's image in the ways in which they have helped the women in these stories "reach for the stars."

Some women have the internal motivation or true grit to achieve without the help of any man, but most women have been shaped by their culture to acquiesce to a secondary role that may never tap into the gifts and abilities they have. In many such cases, women spend their lives chasing the trivial or the ephemeral because they don't know they can do more. What a waste of God's good gifts!

Jesus told a story about a king going on a long journey and entrusting three of his servants with the management of some of his wealth during his absence. Two of the three servants took some risks by investing the wealth for a good return, and they were repaid, first, by success in their investments, and second, by the commendation of the king and the rewards he showered on them. The third servant, however, took no risks

---

1. Marriages break down when any one of these three actions fail. Marriages fail when either husbands or wives fail to "leave" emotionally, as well as physically, their families of origin. Marriages fail when either husband or wife fails to "cleave," to commit to permanence in the marriage "for richer, for poorer, in sickness or in health." And marriages fail when the two fail to see their complete interdependence as "one flesh."

and buried the king's wealth in the ground. When the king returned home and asked for a report on the investments made, he richly rewarded the first two servants. But when the third servant dug up the wealth and returned it to the king, the royal response was devastating: "You wicked, lazy servant! . . . you should have put my money on deposit with the bankers, so that when I returned, I would have received it back with interest. . . . Throw the worthless servant outside, into the darkness, where there will be weeping and gnashing of teeth" (Matt 25:26–30).

God expects women as well as men to use the gifts he gives them. Blessed is the man who sees and seizes opportunities to encourage sisters in God's kingdom to move out and develop, then to use all that God has given them for God's glory. Blessed indeed is the woman who has such a man in her life. We are blessed that Cindy Lathrop and Jewel Hyun have gathered these stories of such men and women for our encouragement.

Alice P. Mathews
Christmas 2009

Preface

And the Lord God said . . . "Hatred I will make between you and
the woman, and between your seed and her seed." . . .
To the woman [God] said . . . "And for your husband
you will be longing, and he will rule you."

GENESIS 3.15–16
(AUTHOR'S TRANSLATION)

ALL OF US ARE familiar with this thoroughly depressing passage of
Scripture from Genesis 3:14–16, called "the curse," where God details the ramifications precipitated by the rebellion of our first parents, or
what we could term the first news report from the front at the opening
hostilities of the war between the sexes. So much misery has followed
down through the ages as women and men reach out to each other only to
find their selfish selves in a battle to take power over the other. The story
of that struggle has blighted history, and it blights so many of our own
lives. It is a tragedy in the classic sense: The character flaw within each of
us of wanting to be god dictates our actions and causes the downfall of
our love for each other. It truly is a tale from the dawn of time that defines
our lives together.

But this book tells a different story entirely—a story of hope and
redemption. It begins with the true God's dramatic intervention in our
misery in the advent of Jesus the Christ, the One sent to us as the anointed
presence of God-Among-Us, who entered our world, broke the cycle of
our power struggle by reminding us of God's prior claim on both halves
of humanity. He redeemed us from the tragic patterns of our rebellion
against God, and therefore against the harmony God intended within
humanity, restored us to obedience to God—and to the gift of unselfish,
sacrificial love for each other, which our first parents had at the beginning

of their lives together—and taught us to love again by the example of first loving us.

Such a book as the one you are holding now could only be written by people living in this armistice declared by Jesus. Hostilities were suspended at his cross, détente has been declared in his resurrection, weapons have been outlawed in his church, and the love of God has been returned to human relations.

Exemplary of the godly women who graciously wrote these chapters in honor of the men who love them are the editors, Jewel and Cindy—two of the most godly women I know. Jewel is a gentle, dignified, brilliant scientist who currently applies her skills to a far-reaching ministry in Africa, supported by her encouraging husband. Cindy is a delightful, caring, loving person whose many children, along with her pastor-husband, rise up and call her blessed. For wholesome, perceptive, godly editors, one could not find any team better. And the remarkable thing about this book is that both independently received the same inspiration to do it within a short time of each other, without knowing the other had been inspired with the same idea. One proposed the book idea to us at the House of Prisca and Aquila right after the other did. Coincidence? We didn't think so. We saw the Spirit of God at work. So, we suggested they pool their resources, and out of that instant camaraderie came this book. It is astounding how rapidly they assembled their authors. Every woman here—leaders all—was eager to tell about the encouraging men in her life.

When I was asked to write this preface, I was humbled, embarrassed, and honored beyond belief that my own wife wanted to tell the story of her father, but include me as well. I wondered if I would feel like the husband in the P. G. Wodehouse's story, whose novelist wife revealed the most intimate details of their romance in her latest tale. But I had nothing to worry about. This book isn't like that. As I read this encouraging, edifying, uplifting set of confessions, I understood this is more than an extended greeting card between two lovers who have finally come to terms with each other's foibles and are at peace in their differences. No doubt it has that dimension as well, but it is about something far deeper: the story of what life can be like when husband and wife are redeemed. It is an account of what happens after spouses experience the restoration in the mission of Jesus Christ, of how human rebellion has been quelled in each heart and the imbalance that caused the man to take control over his beloved by sheer aggression and physical might—and for her desire to love him to be relegated to subjection—has begun to be ended. This is about living life no longer under but back beyond the curse, as my wife has titled her famous book, back to the way God first intended us to live in mutual submission to one another and joint submission together to God.

What you hold in your hand is a book about hope. Expect to be edified and uplifted and to glimpse the possibility in your own home relationship that a little bit of God's intention for harmony within humanity can be restored, thanks to the promise of heaven brought to us by Jesus, the one who lifts up the valleys, brings down the mountains, and makes all the torturously crooked paths of human relationships as straight as God intended.

William David Spencer

Acknowledgments

THE IDEA OF THIS book was conceived by each of us independently during the spring of 2008. We then each consulted Rev. Dr. William David Spencer for guidance. There are not enough words to thank Dr. Spencer for his enthusiasm and encouragement for making our ideas a reality. Dr. Aída Besançon Spencer has been an inspiration as she has guided and advised us from the beginning, always willing to help us with our questions and lead us to the next step.

We are grateful to the staff of the House of Prisca and Aquila for believing in this project and accepting it. From Wipf and Stock Publishers, we thank Jim Tedrick, managing editor, who was our first contact, Diane Farley, the editorial administrator, and we thank Tina Campbell Owens for her patience and skill in typesetting this book. We could not have accomplished this without their professional expertise. Our heartfelt thanks go to Dr. Freeman Barton for editing our first draft, and to Deb Beatty Mel for her copyediting.

We also wish to thank all of the contributors. Without them, this book would not have been possible. Their writing has truly helped us to appreciate what God is doing in the world. We thank them for taking the time to share their stories.

As for those who kept this book project in prayer, we believe that their role was vital and are grateful for their support. To our husbands, our very dear partners, we love and thank them for their encouragement to stay on course and finish the book. Finally, we thank the Lord for guiding us and giving us wisdom and perseverance for the completion of this task. May God receive all the glory!

Cynthia Davis Lathrop, KeumJu Jewel Hyun

Men of Excellence and Women of Endurance
Bring Honor to God

AN INTRODUCTION

KeumJu Jewel Hyun

A KOREAN SAYING, "BEHIND every great man there is a great mother," is commonly brought up when there is news of great achievement paying tribute to the mother's sacrificial devotion to her child's success, even adult child's. The story of Hines E. Ward, Jr., is an example of such a saying when the wide receiver for the NFL's Pittsburg Steelers was voted most valuable player of Super Bowl XL in 2006. The news organizations in Korea were ecstatic in reporting the fact that Ward was born in Seoul, Korea, and that his mother is a Korean, Young Hee Kim. One article had its title, "The secret of Superman Ward's success is the power of his mother's love" (my translation).[1] Other news media reports that a popular Internet café was inundated with comments lauding not just Ward's achievement, but more his Korean mother's sacrificial devotion to Ward, making it possible for him to become such a superstar. When then-president the late Roh Moohyun invited the mother and son to the Blue House,[2] Ward said to the president that he credited his success to his mother's support and sacrifices.[3] Reading such news reports, I was reminded of a similar saying:

1. Hanooki.com, http://sports.hankooki.com/lpage/moresports/200602/sp20060206 17410358130.htm, February 6, 2006.

2. The official residence of the president of South Korea.

3. Hanooki.com, http://news.hankooki.com/lpage/politics/200604/h2006040611282 121080.htm, April 6, 2006.

"Behind every great man there is a great woman." To that, I would make a proposition that behind enduring women there are good men of excellence. Joseph, Jesus' earthly father in the New Testament, is such a man.

Joseph was an extraordinary man for supporting Mary in carrying out the divine mission, which she received from the angel of the Lord. Mary was engaged to Joseph to be married, but before the marriage, she was told that she was carrying a baby conceived by the Holy Spirit (Matt 1:18–25). Since her pregnancy was outside of marriage, according to the Mosaic law, she deserved to be stoned to death as an adulterer. Being an upright man, Joseph did not want Mary be exposed to public dishonor, so he decided quietly to break the engagement. While he was contemplating this plan, he fell asleep; then an angel of the Lord appeared to him in a dream and told him not to be afraid of taking Mary as his wife. The angel explained Mary's task and instructed Joseph to name the child Jesus. When he woke up, Joseph followed what the angel commanded him to do. Joseph married Mary and took her home to be his wife; he named the baby Jesus as he was commanded.

Joseph was a man of faith and knowledge. He was able to discern the voice of the angel of the Lord from that of his own human flesh. He was a man of integrity, keeping his commitment and marrying Mary. In addition, Joseph was a man of obedience; he did exactly what the angel of the Lord had commanded him, even though it could have meant rejection by his friends and family. He took what the angel of the Lord commanded as priority over his own reputation; he knew what was important; he followed God's plan. Although Mary was the focus in the story of the coming of the Messiah, Joseph played a key role as well by supporting her and standing by her. When Jesus was born, both Mary and Joseph played equally important roles as parents. Joseph was Jesus' legal father and legal guardian, and he provided for Jesus. Together, they offered a loving environment where Jesus grew up learning carpentry skills from Joseph during his ministry preparation period. Joseph was an upright man helping a woman, Mary, to carry out what God intended her to do for the human race. What a man he was!

Jesus Christ was a great advocate of women while he was on earth. In first-century Palestine, women were not highly regarded. Stereotypical portrayals of women abound in the writings of Philo and Josephus, in the book of Ben Sira, and in the Mishnah. Women rarely received formal education; the culture defined a woman's primary duty as being a homemaker.

The Mishnah defines the work a woman does for her husband: grinding flour, baking bread, doing the laundry, preparing meals, feeding her children, making the bed, and working in wool.[4] Women were denied the right to bear witness, except in a few limited cases,[5] and the Jewish people were taught that it is better to burn the Torah than to convey it to women.

Compared with these cultural demands and teachings, the attitude of Jesus toward women differs sharply. Jesus treated women positively; he spoke with women in public and demonstrated compassion toward them. Although the Twelve were men, Jesus allowed women to follow him and participate in his ministry; he talked with many women and ministered to them. Throughout the gospels, women are prominent in the narratives of Jesus' birth, crucifixion, and resurrection. All four gospels devote considerable space to Jesus' interactions with women throughout his ministry. From those accounts, we can identify several countercultural ways in which Jesus treated women, including the fact that women were among Jesus' most devoted disciples.

Jesus treated women as equal to men. In Luke 18:9–19, Jesus deals with a despised man and his attitude of the heart in true prayer. From the fact that Jesus used female and male examples in this teaching on prayer, we can see that women are equally valued. When he chooses a woman in need of help as an example, Jesus focuses on the woman's persistence and perseverance as positive characteristics in prayer, although patriarchal society considered those qualities to be negative attributes in a woman.

The story of the healing of the crippled woman (Luke 13:10–17) teaches that Jesus restored dignity to a woman. On a Sabbath day, when Jesus was teaching at a synagogue, a crippled woman entered. For eighteen years, she had been bent over and could not stand up straight. When Jesus saw her, he interrupted his teaching and freed her from her sickness, enabling her to stand up straight in front of everyone. More significantly, he called her "a daughter of Abraham." In the New Testament, there are many references to "children of Abraham" or "seed/descendent of Abraham" (Matt 3:9; Luke 3:8; John 8:33, 37; Acts 13:26; Gal 3:7, 29), but this is the only instance in which "a daughter of Abraham" is referenced. This is significant because it indicates that, although Jewish custom regarded women to be less important than men, Jesus considered this woman to

---

4. *m*Ketubbot 5.5.

5. *m*Yebamot 16.2.

belong to the family of Abraham. Jesus restored not only her physical wholeness, but also her personhood and dignity.

After Jesus' discourse regarding Beelzebub (Luke 11:14–26), a woman was so impressed that she, envying Jesus' mother, wished to have such a son: "Blessed is the mother who gave you birth and nursed you" (Luke 11:27 NIV). Jesus told her that what makes one blessed is hearing his message and responding to it, not motherhood with a son. Jesus corrected this woman's view of her own role as limited to being a mother. He affirmed her personhood, emphasizing her worth beyond her sexuality or other characteristics.

Jesus was willing to teach women and let women be present with men when he taught. Mary, the sister of Lazarus, was one woman who sat before Jesus. In the story of Mary and Martha (Luke 10:38–42), the description that Mary "sat at the Lord's feet and listened to his teaching" is significant because sitting at a teacher's feet and listening meant that a person was a disciple of that teacher. Thus, this account portrays Mary studying as Jesus' disciple. Jesus recognized Mary's choice to study rather than to work in the kitchen, and he affirmed her choice as "really [the] only one thing worth being concerned about. Mary has discovered it— and I won't take it away from her" (Luke 10:42 NLT).

In rabbinic Judaism, women were not allowed to be disciples of a rabbi. A woman gained her knowledge of Torah only through contact in her own home. However, Jesus rejected this rabbinic teaching and let women benefit from his ministry of teaching and healing. Jesus related to Mary in a role that was denied to women: He recognized her capacity to study. In addition, Jesus recognized a woman's full personhood by allowing her to choose her option in her life.

Jesus' discourse with the Samaritan woman in John's gospel (John 4:1–39) is a good example of his countercultural treatment of women. In Jesus' time, Jews and Samaritans did not talk to each other, nor did any Jewish man approach an unknown woman or publicly engage her in conversation, especially a Samaritan woman. The woman by the well, being both a Samaritan and a woman, knew about such customs (John 4:9). Nevertheless, Jesus broke the social and racial conventions of the time and initiated conversation with her, leading her to realize that he was the long-awaited Messiah. He transformed her life; she bore witness to his identity as the Messiah, a testimony that led the people from the village to believe in Jesus (John 4:39). Against all existing social and religious traditions, the Samaritan woman, who was so despised that she could not even come to draw water during the usual hours, led many Samaritan men to Christ; thus, she became the first female evangelist.

Jesus had women disciples. Women as well as men witnessed his teaching and proclaiming the good news of the kingdom of God (Luke 8:1–3). Among the women who followed Jesus were Mary Magdalene, Joanna, and Susanna. The discipleship of these women spans the time from the Galilean ministry of Jesus to his resurrection. These women were the predominant witnesses to Jesus' crucifixion and resurrection. The resurrected Lord, recognizing the women's reliability, instructed them to tell the news of his resurrection. Mary Magdalene, Jesus' mother, the sister of Jesus' mother, and several other women (see Matt 27:55; Mark 15:40; Luke 23:49, 24:10; John 19:25) delivered the news of Christ's resurrection and everything that they witnessed to the Eleven and to "all the rest" (Luke 24:9). However, at first the disciples did not believe the women; they thought what the women were saying was "nonsense" (Luke 24:10–11 NLT). All four gospels record these women's role in God's gospel witness (Matt 28:1–10; Mark 16:1, 8; Luke 24:1–12; John 20:1–18). This is a significant affirmation of women, revolutionary in an era when women were not regarded as valid witnesses. Jesus commissioned women to deliver the news (Matt 28:8ff; Luke 24:8ff); the women were the first to receive the risen Lord's command to proclaim his resurrection, and they obeyed that command. This is God's message that both men and women are credible witnesses and capable messengers of the risen Lord.

Mary of Bethany, Mary Magdalene, Joanna, Susanna, Mary the mother of Jesus, and all these women learned to reorient their traditional roles and set the proper priorities in their lives as they followed Jesus. Ben Witherington sees that following Jesus did not mean that these women needed to abandon their traditional roles, but that their transformed lives redefined their roles for a new purpose. They simply took a disciple's role and served their traditional family with new significance and importance.[6]

Jesus valued women, broke rabbinical traditions concerning women's roles, rejected the cultural tendency to devalue women, and allowed women to participate equally with men in his ministry. Likewise, the Apostle Paul had many women coworkers and supports in his minis-

---

6. Witherington, *Women in the Ministry of Jesus,* 118.

try. However, as time went by and Christianity was shaped into hierarchal institutions, women's roles were less recognized and the Christian male's view of women gradually changed. The church fathers considered women inferior, unintelligent, vain, and weak in mind and character. For example, Augustine believed that woman was created for reproductive purposes. Hermas thought women were representative of evil. Tertullian commented on women as the "devil's gateway." Chrysostom thought man had the "image of God" but woman did not, because the image has to do with authority and only man had the authority. Nevertheless, women shared in the early church persecution and emerged as leaders among those martyred. Perpetua and her slave Felicitas are two examples, and their faith contributed to the growth of the early church.

The medieval church placed enormous emphasis on holding hierarchical office and maintained the church fathers' main ideas on women. Women were considered as gifted with less spiritual insight than men and incapable of serving in Christ's ministry. Aquinas believed woman was created as a subordinate, defective human being, inferior to men, with less intellectual capability. However, women were resilient and did not accept such views; they sought to attain recognition through other means, such as piety and charismatic experiences. Catherine of Siena is most well known among devout women in the Middle Ages. She proclaimed her faith in Jesus Christ, evangelized many prisoners, comforted the sick, and served the poor.

The women in the Reformation era faced extreme difficulty in finding opportunities to serve. While proclaiming the priesthood of all believers, Luther thought women were inferior and "good for nothing" outside of the domestic sphere. He thought that woman's place was at home raising children and performing household chores. While the Reformation granted opportunities for men to serve in significant full-time ministries, it offered women nothing more than the roles of mother and wife. Ironically, at no other time were the opportunities for women to serve as limited as they were during the Reformation period. It seems that the Reformers were influenced by the culture of the time rather than taking their own stance to be countercultural like Jesus and Paul. Still, many women contributed to the advancement of Reformed Christian ministry. For example, Katherine Zell, dedicated to the cause of reform, wrote a preface to and published a collection of hymns and encouraged women to participate in hymn singing in the worship service. She also devoted herself to caring for the sick and the imprisoned.

Colonial views on the nature of women and their behavior in the church came from the writings and sermons of the Puritan ministers from England. Women were treated and viewed as subordinate to men; they were regarded as morally and spiritually "weak," powerful seducers, prone to lying, susceptible to doctrinal error, and in possession of heretical opinions. Some congregations even forbade women to sing in the worship service; however, women received an outpouring of admiration when they lived out their faith by reading, writing, and talking to others about God. Women in the nineteenth century made a great impact on the revival of Christianity. Their moral purity and the examples they set by their lifestyles earned them recognition as being "morally superior." Women's attendance at religious services was so great that, some thought, even the Great Awakenings might not have happened without their attendance.

Throughout church history, women refused to accept their limitations as a barrier or to withdraw from being involved in ministry; they sought ways to respond to their individual callings and actively searched for ways to become involved. For many of these women, their motive was simply to serve instead of seeking official recognition in public ministry.

Today, many women, like their predecessors, face impediments to ministry, whether external or self-imposed, and have limited opportunities to serve. Nonetheless, many others, including the authors of this book, are able to serve their church, ministry organization, businesses, or academic institution because men in their lives believed in them, standing by and behind them so they could fulfill God's calling by utilizing their God-given gifts. These men helped the women become who God intended them to be. A Christian's self-image and self-worth are defined by identifying with Christ, who valued women as persons and treated them with dignity. Women as well as men are new creations in Christ and part of the family of God; they are on the road to Christ-likeness.

In the following chapters, eight women of diverse backgrounds offer a glimpse of how men in their lives emulated Christ's treatment of women and affirmed their lives and ministries. These stories are not intended to be self-serving autobiographies, but to draw a broad picture of the power of a man's role in a woman's life, helping her blossom to her full potential.

The first three chapters tell the stories of women from Congo-Brazzaville, Kenya, and South Africa. A university professor, a ministry leader, and a missionary tell their own stories about how father, husband, brother, and/or pastor helped them. Médine Keener writes about how her late father, brother, and her scholar husband helped her to become a professor today. Judy Mbuga presents the story of how she moved on from homebound mother of five to become a leader of many ministry organizations through the encouragement of her father and husband. Nancy Hudson shares her journey of single mother becoming a missionary with help from many men who offered her opportunities to learn, grow, and serve.

Next, Gwen Dewey, who calls herself a "learning junkie," pays tribute to her husband, pastors, and other men in leadership positions who encouraged her and came alongside her to help her eventually become a graduate university president and globetrotting professor. Chapters five and six are stories of women of European background. Elke Werner from Germany, a well-known women's ministry leader, shares the story of her battle with cancer and her husband's support for her to become who she is today. Cynthia Lathrop, a pastor's wife of Irish heritage at an Italian ethnic church, writes about her upbringing in Irish Protestant culture. She talks about how her father's love helped her to understand God's love.

Jewel Hyun of Korean heritage shares her journey from North Korea to a refugee camp in South Korea, to America, and to Africa. She tells the story of how her father, her husband, and the senior pastor of her former home church made a difference in her life and helped shape who she is today. Finally, Aída Spencer of Dominican heritage writes about how a man can help his wife to become the woman God wants her to be through the story of how she and her husband share responsibilities for the household and for raising their child. In the same way, she has helped her husband to become who God wanted him to be. She stresses the interdependencies of man and woman.

All the authors have had their share of difficulties, but they were resilient. With a strong self-image and confidence in Christ, they did not allow external limitations to hinder them. With help from the men in their lives, they pressed on and became who they are today. I can confidently say that each author is pressing on, forgetting what is behind and marching on "toward the goal to win the prize for which God has called me heavenward in Christ Jesus" (Phil. 3:12–14 NIV).

May God grant you encouragement as you read this book!
To God be the glory!
At dawn 2010

2

Special Men in the Life of a Congolese Professor

Médine Moussounga Keener

WHEN I WAS ASKED to write a chapter for this book, I accepted happily, because I have been influenced positively by men who have shaped me to become who I am today. I owe them a debt of gratitude, and I have told them and shown it by my actions. I have thanked the Lord for bringing these men into my life. But I have wanted to shout my gratitude to the world that everybody might hear it. This book has given me the opportunity to do so, and I am deeply grateful to the editors for allowing me to write this chapter.

I believe every person is a gift from God. While some persons can turn that blessing into a curse in the lives they touch, others help those they contact to grow into beautiful people.

Three men in particular have been a great blessing in my life. Without them, I would not be the woman of God I am today. They are my father, Jacques Moussounga, my big brother, Jacques Emmanuel Moussounga, and my husband, Craig S. Keener. They have had a huge impact in my life, and what I learned from them has shaped me into who I am today in my service to my Lord and Savior Jesus Christ.

PAPA JACQUES[1]

I was born and raised in a small country in the central part of Africa, above the equator, Congo-Brazzaville.[2] I grew up in a society which, at

1. "Papa Jacques" is what everybody affectionately calls my dad.
2. Not to be confused with its massive neighbor, the Democratic Republic of Congo.

the time, still firmly believed that boys were more important that girls. Parents yearned for a male child who would take care of them in their old age, so boys received the priority for schooling, for example, if there was a choice to be made. Not all parents believed that way, however, and I was blessed to be born in such a home.

I was raised in a Christian home by a father and mother who tried their best to serve and honor God. Our father, Papa Jacques, raised us all without differentiating between his sons and daughters.

Papa Jacques himself had grown up in a family where parents practiced preferential treatment of certain children. When his mother died, Jacques was five years old, and his father's other wives did not take care of him. The one he lived with always favored her own children over him. When he was about eleven years old, he lost his father, and after that, Jacques was almost on his own until he met Christ.

Due to a certain extent to this experience and also to his relationship with Christ, when Papa Jacques had a family of his own, he raised his children according to Christian principles and showed no favoritism. One of the ways he did this on a daily basis was to check on all his children, calling us by name and making sure that we were doing all right. Another of his habits was to take one of his children for a walk in the evening. We used to look forward to those walks when each one of us would spend quality time with Papa Jacques and ask him all sorts of questions. I guess another reason we waited anxiously for those walks was that we knew we would get a treat.

That characteristic of my father helped me understand that God cares personally for me, that God is eager for me to spend time on a one-on-one basis with him. When I gave my life to Christ, I started spending time with my heavenly Father, telling him what was in my heart and trying to listen to him. Today, these intimate times with God are a source of peace and renewed strength in my life.

Papa Jacques loved people, and there was no condition attached to his love. His love for me in particular and for us children in general helped me trust God's love. Papa Jacques loved us and trusted us, and his love went hand in hand with good discipline. One incident in my teen years continues to remind me that God loves me and trusts me as his beloved child, so I should love him and trust him back. In 1980, I was in high school in another city; I liked to wear baggy clothes and a hat to try to fit in with the other "cool girls." I did not do everything that they did;

I just liked the clothes. One day, I met a friend of my dad's on the street and greeted him politely as I was taught to. He reprimanded me for wearing "these kinds of clothes" and doing immoral things, and threatened to tell my father. I remember answering him boldly and calmly, saying, "My father trusts me." I was not a bit scared because I knew in my heart that I had not done anything to dishonor my dad. A few months later, when I went home for vacation, I talked to my father about this incident, and he told me that his friend had spoken to him about me. He answered him with these words: "I trust my daughter." My dad's affirmation of his trust in me strengthened my conviction to trust and love God even more and to live in a way that honored my dad. In fact, this is one of the reasons I like to call God "Father"; I feel secure in his love and trust, and when I share Christ with others, I feel comfortable encouraging them to love and trust our heavenly Father.

My dad has always been an upright man, and I started learning the value of integrity through his example. He would not accept bribes; he would not favor some people because of their money or fame. In the 1980s, he worked in a town named Dolisie; he was in charge of overseeing the unloading and renting of merchandise wagons. Many who had held this position before him accepted bribes of various sorts, but Papa Jacques would not. Merchant women tried to seduce him, but he would ignore them. Foreign merchants tried to bribe him too, but to no avail. One day, a Mauritanian merchant came to talk to him about his merchandise wagon scheduled to be unloaded the next day. When he left, he gave my dad 100,000 francs in an envelope "to buy himself some juice." That was a lot of money just for juice, and my parents prayed for God's protection and guidance. The next day, my dad found out that the man's wagon was overloaded. He asked him to pay the fees, but the man told him that it was out of the question since he had bought my dad some juice. After work, my dad went to the Mauritanian merchant's store and gave him back his money saying, "Buy yourself some juice." The next day, the merchant paid the fee of 200,000 francs. This story and others strengthened my faith and my desire to live an honorable life for Christ. The impression my dad made on me was that he was a person whose desire was to honor the Lord gave him the strength to do so. In my life, I try to imitate the good example of Papa Jacques; I try in every way to be a woman of integrity.

In my eyes, Papa Jacques is a man of great faith. Since the day he gave his life to Christ, he has followed him wholeheartedly. Before I gave my life to Christ, I lived by my dad's faith. He talked to God as if talking to a friend. He did not use big words or long discourses; he went straight to the point. His were the shortest prayers I have ever heard, and they were prayed in faith, childlike faith.

While we were living in a small village called Mvouti, one day I was seriously sick with an intense migraine combined with malaria and a very high fever. At the dispensary, the doctor gave me some medicine and an injection in my belly, but I was not getting better. When my dad came home from work during his noon break, he saw that I was worse. He called me to his room and said that he was going to pray for me. He uttered a short prayer that went like this: "God, heal my daughter Médine. Amen." Then he asked me if I trusted him. Of course I trusted him; he was my hero. He told me to go and take a bucket shower. A bucket shower is the coldest one, because that water has been sitting in the bucket usually for the whole night. At the thought of the shower, I started to shiver and felt goose bumps on my skin. But I trusted my dad, and I did as I was told. As soon as my fingers touched the water in the bucket, I was healed. The fever left me; I had no more migraine. It was one of my best showers ever.

Papa Jacques' Christian example impressed me so much that, when it was time for me to make a personal decision for Christ at age fifteen, I decided to receive Christ as my personal Lord and Savior. Since then, my father's legacy has remained with me, and I encourage others to have faith in the risen Savior. I live my life trusting the Lord. Even when I do not understand the circumstances, I trust him and know that, in the end, everything will turn out all right—not always the way I expect, but all right.

Everybody who knows Papa Jacques Moussounga knows that he is not ashamed of the gospel of Jesus Christ. He told us that, when he gave his life to Jesus, he wanted to be a pastor or an evangelist, but God called him to a secular job instead, and he has been faithfully and passionately serving his Savior ever since. My dad has been a deacon in the Evangelical Church of Congo for a very long time, but in my eyes, he has done the work of an evangelist. He has preached the gospel everywhere he has gone, in churches and on a one-to-one basis. He has revived a dying church. When we lived in Mvouti, from 1973 to 1976, my dad helped revive the church there. On Sundays, he sometimes went to neighboring villages to preach. In every town or village where he has lived, he has taken an active part in spiritual retreats and other ministries of the church. In fact, some people thought he was a pastor and would call him "Pasteur Jacques." His children were also associated with his ministry. I remember the summer of 1990, when I went back home for vacation after five years abroad as a student. One Thursday, my dad was scheduled to speak at the weekly Bible study; instead, he came home and told me to speak for him. It was a challenge and an honor for me to talk about God to the men and women who came that night.

Proverbs 14:27 says, "The fear of the Lord is a fountain of life, turning a man from the snares of death."[3] I learned from my dad that the fear of the Lord is liberating and positive. As part of that fear of God, my father taught me to resist sin and flee from it. When I was a student in France, I liked a young man from Congo who wanted to have sex with me first and promised he would marry me afterward. I wrote a letter to my dad and explained to him what was going on. My dad is known for his very short prayers and letters. But this time, he took time to send me a long letter and told me to read about the rape of Tamar in 2 Samuel 13:1–18, especially verse 15 that says, "Then Amnon hated her with intense hatred. In fact he hated her more than he had loved her." In his advice, he pointed out that the fear of the Lord is better than anything else. I will always be grateful to him because his advice saved me from a bad mistake. As I live my life in the fear of the Lord, as I teach others to do the same, I know I have someone to look up to.

Jacques Moussounga is a very happy man. He has a warm smile that makes you feel good, and his laughter is joyful. He has a great sense of humor. But Moussounga Jacques has suffered a lot in his life. He lost his mother at a very young age and his father a few years later. He has suffered from many sicknesses; in his late fifties, he had a stroke. After the stroke, he and his family had to escape a war. In the midst of all this, I only once saw my dad discouraged to the extent of asking for death. He has always entrusted everything to the Lord, trusting him to make a way through the sufferings.

When my father had a stroke in 1996, throngs of people visited him in the hospital. His room was like a sanctuary where people came and prayed. Papa Jacques embodied longsuffering as I imagined the Bible asked us to do. As I watch my dad live for Christ, I am constantly learning

---

3. Scripture citations are from the New International Version.

what it means to follow Jesus no matter what. In 2002, my brother and I interviewed my dad and wrote his biography. This is what he said after having been paralyzed for six years: "For the future, I look to God. I do not plan anything on my own; I commit myself to him. I am with my Lord in my suffering."[4]

Papa Jacques always has the hope of eternal things. He always knows that this world is not the end of us; there is a heaven and a hell. My father taught us not to fear death, but to look forward to being with Christ. Perhaps when he was a young man his hope of eternal life was 80 or 90 percent, but for a very long time now, that hope has been steady at 100 percent. During the war, when we were fleeing for our lives, we realized that we had left his medication and some money on the table. Some of us wanted to go back to get them, but he said, "No." He told us that, if it was time for him to die, then he would go and be with his beloved Lord. We are grateful that he did not die and that the Lord brought him back to the remains of his house. But now that he is weak and sick (ten years after war started in Dolisie, his hometown), he has been telling us over and over that he is ready to go and be with his Savior. He is not afraid to die; rather, he is happy to go home and be with Jesus. Eternal hope gives us dignity in suffering, and I have seen that in my father.

I know where I am going when I die, and I teach others that our life does not end with death. Death is but the transition to an even more wonderful life with Jesus. Because of that hope, I pray and tell others that Jesus is the only way to heaven, and they need to receive him in their hearts as their personal Savior and Lord. If they have, then I encourage them to stand firm, especially when things are tough. Watching my dad's last days is a strong reminder of heaven and a great encouragement, even though the pain of seeing him suffer and of future separation are associated with it.

I love and respect my dad; I am so grateful to have had the parents that I have. I thank God for their lives and positive influence on me. Papa Jacques has impacted me in so many ways that I tell him over and over that my ministry is the extension of his ministry. He is my hero. His teachings, discipline, and life examples have empowered me to work with Christian men in total peace and freedom. His constant support throughout my life has been a strong incentive to anchor my life in Christ and serve him in the church.

4. *Biographie de Papa Jacques*, unpublished document, 18.

JACQUES EMMANUEL MOUSSOUNGA

Growing up in Congo, I had a very wonderful relationship with my brother Emmanuel. That relationship made it easy for me to relate to male friends and men in the church.

Dr. Jacques Emmanuel Moussounga is my only older brother (I have two younger brothers and two sisters). Emmanuel is a very intelligent and sensible man who deeply fears the Lord. When we were children, we had our moments of rivalry, fighting and making up, bonding with and appreciating one another, like any other siblings.

As a child, I felt protected by my parents from outside dangers. But when I started going to school, I felt alone sometimes and vulnerable. My brother Emmanuel started standing up for me and defending me whenever other kids took advantage of me, and he gradually became my "superman."

God taught me a lot of things through my friendship with Emmanuel, especially how to relate to persons of the opposite sex. As I entered the tween years (that age when one is too old to be a child and too young to be a teenager), I looked to my brother for protection. I remember how, in sixth grade, our last grade in elementary school, we had to take a national exam in order to go to middle school. I was one of the youngest students in my class and in the group of villages with elementary schools. Most of the students started school late, and by the last year of elementary school, many were teenagers who struggled to understand the courses. On the day of the exam, students from all the neighboring villages came to our village to take all the tests, which then were corrected by teachers and proclaimed at the end of the day. Some of the big boys in my class, who knew that I was a very good student, told me that they would beat me if I did well and passed the exam. I guess that they were jealous that a younger person, and a girl at that, could do better than they and pass.

I knew my brother Emmanuel had promised to come cheer for me at school, which was at about two and a half miles from our house. Having his promise, I knew I would be safe, so I gave my best for my exam, confident that God would help me succeed. Around 4:00 p.m., all the kids, some parents, friends, and passersby gathered around the principal for the public announcement (in alphabetical order) of those who passed the exam. As the principal started calling the names, the big boys hovered over me threateningly. I was scared and anxious because I did not see my brother, and I knew that, if he had left the house late, unless he ran all the way to school, he would never make it on time to hear my name. As a consequence of his absence, not only would I not rejoice in my success, but I would be beaten because of it; I could not escape those bullies.

As the principal continued to call names, I thought my pounding heart could be heard by the whole group. Then the principal began calling names starting with M (like my last name). I knew then that I was going to get the beating of my life. About a minute or two before I heard my name, I saw Emmanuel coming. I ran toward him and told him that the big boys were going to pound me if my name was on the list, to which he replied, "Let them try!" Then we heard, "Moussounga Médine," and I shouted with joy, "Yes, yes, yes!" Emmanuel and other friends cheered for me. Then my brother, who was younger than some of those big boys, faced then and called out, "Who is first?" They all ran away. That day, as I came home with my brother, running, laughing, and shouting, "Hooray," Emmanuel became one of the few people I counted on. He taught me two things that day: Always try to stay true to your word, and stand up for those you love. As I look back on that day, I know that some young men, like those bullies, are mean and wicked, but others, like Emmanuel who risked his life to help me, are brave and trustworthy. From that day on, I have tried to stay away from malicious and unkind men and to trust thoughtful and caring men.

In October 1982, I started my first year of college at Marien Ngouabi University in Brazzaville; Emmanuel was then a sophomore. We rented a two-bedroom apartment together. Emmanuel and I each had a monthly scholarship of 62 US dollars (30,000 francs). We did not have any other financial help, yet we decided to take in six other students who had no scholarship and provided them with lodging and/or food at no cost. We did this during our three years of undergraduate studies. I consider these to be three formative years. My brother and I became very close and shared all responsibilities equally. We were on fire for the Lord and were eager to serve him and others with all our hearts.

I learned to trust Emmanuel even more and open up to him; he became my closest friend. As we were helping those in need without expecting anything in return, we learned not to fear responsibility, but to discern priorities, and what is good and bad. We also learned to have pure and healthy relationships with friends of the opposite sex. God was teaching me to love and serve others for Christ's sake. Through this experience with Emmanuel, I discovered God's caring heart for his people.

I remember how Emmanuel and I prayed every time we received our meager scholarship, then we put our financial contribution for housing, food, and other needs into envelopes. We then sought God personally for guidance with the remaining francs. These were wonderful experiences of depending on the Lord, of opening our hearts and apartment to those who were not part of our biological family, and inviting them to come and share in the little that we had. I was part of a small ministry to students and friends who had no scholarship. I don't think I could have done it by myself. But together with my brother, we served Christ by serving others. Emmanuel, without knowing it, reinforced in me what I had learned at home: to serve Christ by serving others. My brother's friendship also helped me to set boundaries in my relationships.

While doing our undergraduate studies, Emmanuel and I taught children's Sunday school in two different districts of Brazzaville among two different ethnic groups. We talked a lot about our ministry and shared our praises and concerns for the kids. Because we were seen together by the children and their parents, and they could feel that we loved one another, the children in our two very different groups started to build friendships and love one another. That was an amazing discovery for me: that our actions sometimes speak louder that our words. And because the children were from different ethnic groups, we were building bridges for ethnic reconciliation.

I remember one encounter with a mother who tried to rebuke us for having a friendship that would mislead her children. She thought that the only friendship possible between a young woman and a young man had to do with dating and sex. We told her that we were siblings, but she did not believe us until we showed her our ID cards. She apologized profusely and recognized that pure relationships between people of the opposite gender were possible. Our sincere prayer was that our example would teach the teenagers to forge pure and healthy relationships.

Jacques Emmanuel Moussounga is a trustworthy man. I had known that through the years, but this knowledge was bolstered during my stay in the United States. Money has divided many friends and families, wherever there is no trust. When I came to the United States as an exchange student, I entrusted all my bank information to my brother so that he could take care of my bank account and make sure that whatever money I received was put into my account. Some of my friends thought I was crazy and would end up having tension and maybe conflict with my brother. I told them that I trusted Emmanuel as he trusted me. Emmanuel took good care of my bank account.

With Emmanuel, I learned to experience these things: "Help one another," "Serve one another," "Trust one another." I discovered that a relationship without trust is doomed to failure. So, when I work with men (and women) in the church, I like to have a trust-based relationship where we have the freedom to serve the Lord with the gift he has given us, bringing my input and sharing in whatever ministry I am part of. I knew of ministers taking advantage of women, but I was not afraid because I had learned from my brother where to set boundaries and how to express myself. Emmanuel's friendship taught me to have unassailable relationships with male friends. I am grateful to the Lord for my brother's friendship and love.

CRAIG KEENER

The first time I set foot on American soil was in August of 1989. I was a doctoral student from the Republic of Congo, studying African American history in Paris, France. I needed to come to the United States for research. I applied for a scholarship and was turned down. I was told that the scholarship was for French students first. When I received the letter telling me that I was not accepted, I felt devastated, since I had done well on my test. Deep inside, I believed that God was going to open that door for me, even though my faith was very low on the issue. So I called my dad in Congo and asked him to pray that God would open a door for me. I needed a miracle. I was too discouraged to even give my father the details of my situation, but he promised to pray for me.

A week after my refusal letter, I received another letter from the same university office informing me that I had been granted a scholarship to study in the United States. I rejoiced and praised God for opening that door. I believe what probably happened was that the United States had a student ready to come and study in France, but since most French students liked to go to England, there was not one to send to the States. I then was given the scholarship to study in the United States. Little did I know that, in this exchange program, I was going to meet a young man who would have such a tremendous impact on my life. Little did I know that, through him, God was going to answer one of my most gripping prayer requests at the time: "Lord, give me a husband who knows you, loves you, and serves you with all his heart and who will love me too."

In Congo, and later on in France, I was always involved in *Groupes Bibliques Universitaires,* the French equivalent of InterVarsity Christian fellowship (IVCF). So, when I got settled at Duke University as an exchange student, and my English became good enough for me to communicate, I looked for and joined the IVCF chapter on campus. I became very active in the undergraduate chapter of IVCF and in the International Christian Fellowship, and participated in Christian outreach on campus and out of state. One day, I heard about the graduate chapter of IVCF and wanted to attend the meeting. The person who was speaking that day was a New Testament doctoral student named Craig S. Keener. Craig was a handsome, slender young man of great intelligence and learning. He spoke on the gift of the Holy Spirit. But the thing that struck me the most that day was his uncommon zeal for the Lord. He looked like a man at peace with God, although he also seemed sad.

Craig had a cloud over him, some kind of sadness that I could feel, yet he was full of love for and devotion to God.[5] That sadness did not destroy his faith in and love for Jesus. I took courage from his experience. As an international student, I had many difficulties including homesickness, a language barrier, and loneliness. But seeing Craig's life encouraged me to seek God always and with all my heart. He reinforced in me something that my parents taught me: In the midst of your trials, always bring everything to God, because God is everywhere.

Another way I would describe Craig is by quoting Paul's statement in Romans 1:16: "I am not ashamed of the gospel, because it is the power of God for the salvation of everyone who believes." I was impressed by Craig's passionate evangelizing heart. Every time I saw him on campus, he was full of love for God and for other people. He seized every opportunity to share his faith or encourage someone in the Lord. I was encouraged in my own witnessing not to be ashamed of the gospel of Jesus Christ.

As an international student, I came across people from different backgrounds, nationalities, and races. In Congo, I experienced tribalism, which is a form of racism; in France and the United States, I experienced racism. But Craig and other brothers and sisters showed me that God

5. I did not know at that time that Craig was going through one of the biggest crises of his life.

does not show favoritism to any one group of people; instead, his love is for all peoples. Every time I was with Craig, I saw him bless fellow students with a "God bless you," and a genuine smile. Craig's treatment of others reinforced in me the decision to treat others with grace and understanding. My parents taught me to love and serve people for Christ, which I always tried to do with God's help. Craig's example reinforced that notion and took it to a global level. I felt the strength to continue to serve Christ in a cross-cultural way and to try to understand those who were different from me.

At the end of my eight and a half months at Duke University, Craig had become a very close friend. As I left North Carolina for France, I knew that I had friends who not only cared for me, but would also pray for me, friends I cherished in my heart—and Craig Keener was one of them. Craig and I kept in touch, mostly through mail and occasionally by phone. Craig's example continued to influence me in a positive way. He taught me a lot in our correspondence, because every time I had a question about the Bible or the Christian life, I asked him. He always took time out of his busy schedule to answer my questions. As the months and years passed, besides my brother Emmanuel, Craig became my closest male friend. He knew my hopes and fears and prayed for me.

My relationship with my brother had helped me have a good relationship with young men in general as I was growing up. But some men, including some of my professors at the University of Brazzaville, made it difficult for me to trust men readily. A certain number of them behaved as if the only possible relationship between a man and a woman was sexual. Craig's pure heart and friendship was a welcome change. Craig helped me rediscover that a genuine friendship between people of opposite sex is possible. I realized that, in Christ, we have a treasure of relational communication that is very beautiful. Craig's friendship made me a strong Christian woman; I knew better whom and when to trust. Craig helped me to be "wise like a serpent and innocent like a dove" when dealing with some men in or outside the church.

Craig was a great source of blessing in my personal life and ministry. As a student in France, I was engaged in open-air and door-to-door evangelism, and I continued to teach children in Sunday school. He blessed me beyond measure by his constant "coaching" and teaching. He was like a mentor from a distant land.

But Craig blessed me in other areas too. As I strived to finish my Ph.D., Craig was always encouraging me. He supplied me with books and articles on African American history. At one point, I thought of giving up and looking for a job or going as a missionary to some country. My friend Craig Keener exhorted me to complete my dissertation. He was the first person to point out to me that a Ph.D. would be a great asset for God in reaching the lost. A doctorate would give me access to students, fellow professors, and the intellectuals who would not listen to me if I did not have a doctorate. I had not really thought in those terms. But the more I did think about it, the more I became convinced that Craig was right; God was going to use this degree for his glory if I let him. Reaching out to intellectuals in my country would mean reaching out to the "cream" of my people, some of them decision makers. The Ph.D. was a challenge and a blessing, and God used Craig to open my eyes to this very important aspect of my life: my ministry as an educated African woman. For years, I taught children in Sunday schools and had been involved in youth ministry. But now, it seemed a new door was opening up before me for Christ. Craig's words encouraged me so much that I continued to work on my dissertation and completed it in 1993.

My time back home was very busy and enlightening. Working as an adjunct at the University of Brazzaville and as an English instructor at the English language program of the American embassy, I had many opportunities to be a witness for Christ and was happy to be of use to my Lord with my students and colleagues. After a series of sad circumstances connected to a civil war in which I ended up as a refugee for eighteen months, God did a great miracle for me. I got in touch again with my friend Craig. We were married in March 2002. Since our wedding, I have been blessed even more by God and through Craig.

When people see Craig Keener from a distance, perhaps they see an intensely disciplined scholar whose life seems to be consumed by his writing. But when they get to know him, they discover a deeply sensitive, humane man of God. He is a kind and loving husband, a good father, and an excellent teacher. Craig Keener is a keen, intelligent, and hardworking New Testament scholar, but most of all, he is a humble devoted servant of the Lord Jesus Christ. Living out his calling is not easy, yet it is far from boring or dull. Life is full of adventures and lessons to learn. Since the One who called him called me too, we have been walking in this exciting and sometimes challenging journey together. Being married to Craig has helped me learn and/or reaffirm some very important lessons in my life as a servant of the Lord. I have seen and heard of scholars who have the help of their students to write their books. Currently, Craig does not have anyone to help him. He works alone from start to finish in his writing projects. Sometimes, I am afraid that he works too hard, especially when he starts to index in his sleep! He did this especially during his work on the Gospel of John commentary, working at indexing the two-volume commentary sixty hours a week for four months. I know he is compelled by the desire to serve his Lord and reach out to others, so I come alongside to help in any way I can. By so doing, I am reminded to work hard myself in my teaching and mentoring students here and there, teaching Sunday school and exercising the gift of hospitality.

I met Craig when he was not yet the famous scholar that he is today, and I can say that his heart has remained humble. I am grateful that I started learning my lesson in humility in a very dramatic way, during the civil war in Congo. I was stripped of all material possessions, health, and even my marriage.[6] Craig's humble heart has reinforced the notion of humility that God began to teach me, and I try to teach those who come in touch with me about humility and the blessing that we can receive from it.

Craig Keener is a God-fearing man. All he desires is to please the Lord and do what is right in his sight. Proverbs 9:10 says, "The fear of the Lord is the beginning of wisdom." As I see the way my husband reveres Jesus, I am stretched in my awe of God. One of the first verses I memorized was John 3:16: "For God so loved the world that he gave his one and only son, that whoever believes in him shall not perish but have eternal life." In response to that perfect and wonderful love of God, I love and respect him back, witnessing to those I encounter by my words and deeds. That respectful, fearful admiration and love for our Savior is liberating and fulfilling. And as I watch my husband daily express the "wise fear" of the Lord, as he calls it, my own intimacy with God is strengthened and renewed, and God's love is poured out to the people I meet.

I have lived simply, in dire circumstances, at times surviving only on bread and water, but I must say that Craig's commitment to living simply touched me. Craig has always lived sacrificially for his heavenly Father. Many people sacrifice by feeding the poor, helping the sick, spon-

---

6. During the war, many married women were abandoned by their spouses because of political, tribal, moral, or other reasons; I was one of them.

soring orphans and poor children mainly in the Majority World.[7] We are all serving God in various ways. God has given Craig a strong passion to train and educate God's people. Hosea 4:6 says, "my people are destroyed from lack of knowledge." Craig's passion is to give God's people the scriptural word in its context so that they will live and prosper. Before he got married, Craig gave 90 percent of his total income to those in need and sent books to the Majority World so that God's people might be equipped to serve him better. He lived in a small apartment and ate simple food to accomplish this.

When I married him, Craig explained to me how he had been living, how all his writing income went back into serving God's people through the books. I agreed with him, but did not understand him at first. I prayed about it, and the Lord opened my heart to see Craig's greatness of heart for others. Since then, I have embraced this ministry wholeheartedly.

Craig has taught me that we should care not only for physical, emotional, and moral needs, but for spiritual needs as well, including training God's people in the word. I remember how shocked I was during my time in France to see that Christians had access to commentaries and other edifying materials while, in my country, pastors with Bible commentaries were rare. I was touched that my people did not have the proper tools to study the word of God. Now I see that, through us and many others, God is providing materials for those who usually cannot afford it so they will be equipped to teach God's people.

Sending books is backbreaking, time-consuming, and financially costly. We sacrifice a lot, but we are grateful to be able to make a small difference for Christ. The many e-mails that Craig receives concerning the positive impact of those books in people's lives and in God's church, are a great reward for our hearts. This ministry connects to my desire to touch the intellectuals in my country and all of Africa. I have been happy to contribute in this ministry by translating some of Craig's books into French so that the francophone countries in Africa and elsewhere can benefit from his scholarship. So we live simply to bless others, trusting God to take care of our needs.

When I came to this country out of a war-torn Congo, I felt lost. I needed healing from the wounds of the war and from some of the experiences of my past. I had to survive in my new culture and environment.

---

7. We do support some of these ministries.

At times, I did not feel like serving God in the ways he had used me in the past, let alone attempt to serve him in new ways. I was content to be a mother and a wife and to do my job. It was my husband who first started to nudge me gently to use my God-given talents to serve his people. I resisted him for a while, too afraid to try anything. I remember when Craig strongly encouraged me to speak at the Christians for Biblical Equality conference at Eastern University in July of 2005. I agreed very reluctantly and went forward trembling like a leaf on the day of my presentation. Yet, when I started to speak, I felt God's peace and strength. Encouraged, I talked about the need of my people and shared many stories about women in Congo-Brazzaville. After the conference, I felt happy, as if the Lord were telling me, "You did well, daughter, you did well." Now, as I teach college students, teach Sunday school, speak about the needs in Africa or war in the Congo, and exercise the gift of hospitality, I know my husband is praying for me and I feel encouraged and affirmed in my ministry. Whenever he can, he comes to listen to me, and when I see him in my audience, I thank God for sending this fine man to be my husband and for the positive influence that he has in my life. Craig is my friend, my brother in Christ, and my dear husband, and I love him very much.

I am the person I am today in part because of these three men and their positive influences in my life. God has used their love and continuous encouragement to forge me into the woman of God I am today. A positive relationship with persons of the opposite sex is a wonderful blessing. Because of the lives of these three men and the positive impact they have had in my life, I have been able to work side by side with men in God's kingdom, feeling comfortable that they are God's gift to his people, as I am.

Editor's note: Papa Jacques went home to be with the Lord just a few days after the author had completed her chapter. The following is her tribute.

Papa Jacques passed away Saturday, July 4, 2009.

Papa Jacques was a faithful, affectionate, and devoted husband to his wife and a loving father to his children. He spent a lot of time with us, instructing us in the ways of life and in God. He showed us the way to salvation and strengthened our steps in the Lord. Each one of us had the opportunity many times to confide in him unreservedly.

Papa Jacques was not perfect, but he is the best dad in the whole world to me and my siblings, and we love him wholeheartedly. We have lost a father, a counselor, a guide, and unquestionably a friend.

I know that one day I will see him and live with him (and with many others) always in the presence of God. Happy home-going, Papa Jacques, and see you soon in heaven. I love you, Papa.

Your daughter, Médine

3

Men Who Have Greatly Influenced My Life

Judy W. Mbugua

MY FATHER, HOSEA WAINAINA

Father's Day is celebrated in many countries in the world once a year. I appreciate the way my children come out on this day to honor their father for his role as parent to them. On these occasions, each of my children has a surprise gift for their father, and they keep thanking him for being the best dad they know. On this day, I often find myself preoccupied with two thoughts. First, I am challenged and have a longing to spend each day with the heavenly Father expressing my gratitude and love to God. He is the perfect Father whose love can only be experienced and not explained. Second, my children's love for their father triggers memories of my own dad, Hosea Wainaina. Back in our day, Father's Day was unheard of and, had it been celebrated, then every day would have been Father's Day to me. There is a Kenyan folk saying that goes like this: "A child always thinks what his parents require of him is old-fashioned, until he grows up and has children who think what he requires of them is old-fashioned."

True to this, my siblings and I would often brush away our father's expectations as too strict or too unfair. Sometimes, in the spirit of rebellion or mischief, we found ourselves going against his instruction. My father was not willing to give up on us so easily, or maybe spare the rod and spoil us. He was determined to give us a holistic upbringing. He endeavored to have us well-rounded in Christian faith, academic excellence, and good discipline to become people who would fit in the society. Knowing well that children are poor listeners and good imitators, dad and mum acted as good role models to us.

Daddy, whose rest time came nineteen years ago, was and still is my icon of determination and zeal for excellence. Dad went to school as a result of abduction by the colonial masters, who wanted to give some African boys the opportunity to receive an education. The parents of the boys did not take to this kindly, as they felt that their herds of cows and goats would be left unattended. They also felt this was further colonial intrusion into their private lives. Consequently, only the fatherless like my dad were taken to school. Dad went through the prestigious Alliance High School (one of the best-performing schools in Kenya today).

Dad was a staunch Christian. He ensured that we joined Sunday school, church, and morning worship. Later on in the evening, as we sat around the fireplace waiting for mum to prepare dinner, he would question deeply what we had learned from Sunday school. He also expected us to pray before retiring to bed. From an early age, we learned to speak to our heavenly Father. Sometimes we got curious to know who this heavenly Father was. Daddy patiently explained.

During the fight for independence in Kenya, the freedom fighters did not like those who had taken on the white man's religion. As a result, dad's position of faith threatened his life and the lives of the entire family as the Mau Mau (freedom fighters) sought to take away his life. Every night, he had to sleep in the good chief's post while the rest of the family hid in the maize plantations. He insisted we talk to our God, who would protect us, and God surely did.

Back then, our culture did not encourage education for girls. It was considered irrelevant, since the girl would eventually get married and be detached from the rest of the family. The old folks considered it wiser to educate the girl on household chores that would be of value to her later on in marriage. When she was of age and skillful in homemaking, she would attract suitors who would bring large herds of cattle. Going to school back then was seen as a way of introducing the young mind to the white man's way of life, which was largely contradictory to the African traditions. Formal education was therefore dismissed as an intention by our colonizers to make the girls hardheaded and rebellious. There was fear it was of more harm than good.

My learned father had no place for this cultural perception about girls. He was against the norms. He instead encouraged me to work as hard as the boys were doing in school. I remember vividly walking to the school alongside him on chilly mornings prior to my joining school. Probably he was preparing me for what was to come. Later, I walked to school barefoot with prickly thorns along the way. It was the cost of living with an educated father. He foresaw the positive outcome. Later on, when I overlooked higher education in favor of my marriage to my then boyfriend and now dear husband, it was a bitter pill for my dad to swallow. Dad seriously valued education, and that greatly impacted us. I had no excuse; he was willing to pay the cost of my education. I went back to school as a mother of five children, and now I have been awarded two honorary doctorates: one in ministry and the other in theology. During both ceremonies, I wished my dad were there to see his girl and to know that his work was not in vain.

It would be difficult and unfair if I failed to mention the discipline that my father instilled in his children. I have always thought that Dad must have been very familiar with the Scripture, "Train a child in the way he should go, and when he is old he will not turn from it" (Prov 22:6 NIV). Though at times I would stumble, I always found myself going back to the way I had been taught: the way of hard work and pressing on. Dad was faithful to correct us by word of counsel or by cane.

MY HUSBAND, RICHARD MBUGUA

I am now counting my forty-sixth year since I fell in love and married Richard. I met him when I was serving as an untrained teacher and had taken my pupils out for a school tour to the railway station, where he was working. While the children went to see how the trains operated, I was talking to the station master. I had read Denise Robins' romantic books, which told of meeting Mr. Right, who would be six feet tall and very handsome. Her description of a handsome man fell short of what I found in Richard. He was all I hoped for plus more. He also says he felt the same about me. Ours was love at first sight.

By the time of my marriage to Richard, I was in my late teens. My assumption was that life would be a bed of roses from then on. It turned out to be different. I encountered a number of challenges right from the word go. For instance, ironing my husband's clothes was an uphill task for me. I did not have any prior experience, since mum had always ironed Dad's clothes, and going to school denied me the chance to train in such basic chores. Simple chores like ironing were expected of any woman entering marriage. As a matter of fact, if a wife was considered ineffective with the basic chores, she risked being divorced on the basis of needing to be "taught." However, Richard taught me how to go about it. He also taught me how to manage money. Often, I would run out of finances before the end of the month. Fortunately, my husband always came in to assist with more money. This was not because he had a lot of money, but because he was giving me time to learn, and with time, I did. An ideal wife was expected to be a perfect homemaker. In my case, I was blessed to have patient Richard, who was kind enough to teach me these basics.

When I decided to continue with further education, my husband paid for it in addition to meeting the other family needs. This was not out of abundance, but he did so sacrificially to help me achieve my dreams. He even promised to pay my university fees should I consider going to the university. I trained partially as a secretary, and I was employed to work with the Ministry of Finance. My stay there was marked with promotions and consequent salary increases. The policy was to receive a salary raise after passing all the exams. I worked hard day and night, with crying babies, keeping myself awake by putting my feet in a basin of cold water. This yielded results, and I passed all my secretarial exams in a record two years, making a transition from a copy typist to a top secretary. At one time, I served as the personal assistant to then–minister of finance and Kenya's current president, his Excellency Mwai Kibaki. Later on, I moved to the insurance industry, where I attained the position of the first administration manager. My pleasant job and lucrative salary might cause any husband to feel threatened, but not Richard. Instead, he encouraged me to keep moving up the ladder. He is still my best friend, one of the best fathers, and a man of great confidence. To this day, Richard has kept true to our friendship. He has firmly stood by my side to smile when I smile and wipe my tears when I cry. Continually, he has encouraged me to let the will of God be done in my life.

MY PASTOR, REV. DENNIS WHITE

My passion to serve God, particularly in homes, started soon after I was saved. After our marriage in 1965, the first thing I did was to pray for my family to know the Lord. All my children accepted the Lord at a tender age, but I was praying that all of us, including my husband, would be born again. I had already shared how Richard was and is good to us, but I knew that, without salvation, even though he was that good, he would not receive eternal life. Thus, I purposed to pray for him and thought his salvation would come soon.

It took a long while before my husband accepted the Lord, and this made me a bit lonely in church circles. The pastors would call people for couples' meetings, and I would not attend because my husband would not be willing to come. Then, there would be meetings called for single parents and widows, which, of course, I would not go to since I did not belong to either of these categories. This made me feel very lonely.

One day, when the pastor called for such meetings, I felt so lonely that I almost cried. Then, I felt a gentle whisper telling me that there is no room for self-pity. I felt instructed to look around and see how many other women within our church were in the same situation as I, and I counted about twenty. I felt instructed to invite them to my home for fellowship, which I did. We had a wonderful meeting and decided to repeat it once every month. We also opened it to our friends. By the next meeting, forty women attended.

Ladies Homecare Spiritual Fellowship

This continued on and on and within two years, we had more than three hundred women meeting. We rotated homes, but could no longer fit in any compound. We had moved from inside homes to pitch tents outside the compound, but even this was no longer adequate. We requested permission to meet in church. This was the birth of the Ladies Homecare Spiritual Fellowship (LHSF). In 1985, this fellowship was registered with the government of Kenya after meeting for almost five years in homes and in the church compound. We felt the need to register because it was interdenominational and more women from different churches were attending. The Lord confirmed that I should go on and register the fellowship. Soon after I received the certificate of registration, I was due to depart for an international women's conference in the United States. Because of this, I did not have time to share the joy of the successful registration with many people, including my pastors.

After my return, many people were not happy with the registration, and many untrue stories were told. I was also feeling the call to serve God on a full-time basis, and I needed someone I could really trust for advice.

While still in this dilemma, I took advantage of a four-day retreat organized by one of our church's focused group ministries at Mombasa, Kenya. One afternoon, my pastor, Dennis White, shared on the topic, "God is a speaking God." This message touched my heart. That is exactly what I was looking for: a speaking God. My prayer then became, "God, speak to me." Later that evening, a young lady, sensing a message about me from the Lord, said that the Lord, "has a ministry that Judy will head." The message was clarified that it was God's ministry, a ministry for women, and that he was in control.

On hearing this message, I discussed it with Pastor White, who was also there when the prophecy was given. His encouragement and advice was precious. It propelled me to fulfill God's will for my life. Pastor White prayed for me and separated me for the work of the ministry. This was in April 1988. Although at this time neither my church nor Ladies Homecare Spiritual Fellowship was in a position to support me financially (and I was receiving a very good salary), Pastor White encouraged me to follow the way of the Lord and serve in the women's ministry. Leaving a top job that I had worked hard to attain was not easy, but by God's guidance and continued assurance, I resigned and left not knowing where my next salary would come from.

Looking back, I appreciate my pastor's good advice and continuous encouragement. Homecare has been a source of transformation for many families. Just recently, Sister Elena[1] testified of how the Lord had caused her to marvel by changing her husband. She testified that she had always written her husband's salvation as the priority issue in the prayer requests box at fellowship prayer meetings. Her husband, she said, used to stay up to late into the night on drinking sprees and then come home to beat her up badly. She knew that reporting him to the police would not be of much help, and thus decided to report him to heaven. After prayer, he is now going home early and complaining that his friends drink too much until late in the night. He is also now insisting on family prayers every night before retiring to bed. All glory to God.

Programs to Assist Women and Families

Ladies Homecare Spiritual Fellowship is both a movement and a membership organization with members spread through twenty-one branches.

---

1. Not her real name.

Their vision is to impact families through prayer, evangelism, and social transformation. Toward this vision, we strive to create, develop, and sustain institutional programs and structures that will mobilize, train, and empower families. Among the fellowship's programs are HIV and AIDS assistance for the affected and infected. This program supports thirteen families with a total of one hundred people, and has graduated the first batch of twenty women and seventy children. Homecare supports them with food and clothing, home-based care, school fees for the children, funeral expenses, counseling, group therapy, and medical support. LHSF has started a bead-making project where women make ornaments such as necklaces and bangles to earn a living. Rhoda, who is HIV-positive, was on the verge of committing suicide when she happened to see the LHSF sign board on the road and decided to come in. Our HIV coordinator counseled her and prayed with her. Today, Rhoda is strong and doing well in business.

LSHF started the Kuwinda Dressmaking Project in 1997 after fire gutted the Kuwinda slums in Karen, near the Nairobi city center. Here, dressmaking training is given to youth, and so far two hundred young people have graduated with the government trade test in dressmaking. Upon graduation, each graduate is awarded a sewing machine to make it possible to start their own businesses.

The Mentors, Orphans, and Vulnerable Children program was started in partnership with churches located within Kibera to alleviate poverty, provide education, and empower the caregivers. The key activities are to provide nutritional, educational, and psychosocial support. Sixty-seven children are now going to school under this program with the support of a partner from United States.

I am able to do all this because of a pastor who saw beyond the local church needs and appreciated that God calls beyond that. Thank you, Pastor White.

FULL-TIME MINISTRY: TUKUNBOH ADEYEMO

As I had shared earlier, moving to full-time ministry from a well-paying job was not a decision that I made overnight. My dilemma produced fear about how I would raise my support. Again, for the Lord to confirm that he was calling me for his work, he connected me with my former boss and former secretary general of the Association of Evangelicals in Africa

(AEA), Dr. Tukunboh Adeyemo. When you talk of men of faith, I think of Dr. Adeyemo. I served under him for fifteen years, and I know that he is truly a man of faith. He is also a man who hears from God. At a time when many ministries in Africa would not entrust leadership roles to women, Dr. Adeyemo invited me to AEA to join and lead a major new women's ministry.

In 1988, I traveled to Zambia at the invitation of Dr. Adeyemo to attend the AEA general assembly. At this time in the organization's development, they needed to establish a commission to deal with women's affairs. The twenty-six women present requested that I chair the deliberations. The team worked successfully on the three main agendas, and the Pan-African Christian Women's Alliance (PACWA) was born. What remained was to elect the chairperson of the commission's executive committee. My name came up, and I resisted unsuccessfully. This position had a lot of responsibility to go with it. Considering I was employed, I thought it would put me in an awkward position with my employer, since it would require a lot of off duties. I felt it was inappropriate to take up this position at this particular time, and again, I resisted unsuccessfully. As the chairperson of PACWA, and working in the insurance industry, my mind was always preoccupied with thoughts about PACWA. I longed to see its success. I believed in my heart I should lay a good foundation for the person who would become its next leader. In the meantime, I decided to resign my job by December 1987, but as much as I tried to write the resignation letter, I could not.

PACWA is a movement whose purpose is to bring together leading evangelical Christian women from the whole of Africa to examine the national, continental, and worldwide issues that affect women in the course of their lives. PACWA's theme, derived from Luke 22:28, is a call on women in Africa to unite our efforts to reach the continent of Africa for the Lord Jesus. To this day, PACWA is the women's commission of AEA. I have come to realize that PACWA is the women's ministry the Lord intended to identify me with when he talked with me about ministry. Taking the leadership position of PACWA is the result of the prayers and confidence that Dr. Adeyemo had in me. Dr. Adeyemo knew I had not acquired a university degree, but I had extensive training and experience in leadership and management, both locally and overseas. He accepted me to work in this capacity and promised to pray for me in addition to offering his personal assistance and that of AEA—a promise he kept.

In the past 100 years of church history in Africa, nothing like PACWA has ever taken place. Yet, women are not only the majority in churches in Africa, but they are also the most committed and active members. Women bring energy and enthusiasm in God's work that is unequalled by any other segment of the church, at least in Africa. PACWA is set to address some of the issues not addressed by various other institutions, as their systems and curricula are tied to the male-dominated history of many African countries. PACWA tries to encourage the role of Christian women, and it is also expected to enhance a family spirit for evangelical women in Africa. The objectives of PACWA are:

1. To carry the gospel light to our people who are yet to be reached.

2. To stop the tide of ungodly secularism and materialism.

3. To assert the true dignity of women as found in God's word.

4. To inject biblical morals and values to African society through women who are mothers of all societies.

5. To educate women on matters of justice, equity, and social-economic development.

6. To deliver Africa from moral decadence and ultimate collapse.

7. To foster effective cooperation of all Christian women ministries in Africa.

PACWA's programs are:

1. Networking: Identifying women ministry models, coworkers, and resource people in each country/region.

2. Social-economic issues: Identifying major regional issues and publishing reports to be distributed to various national committees for use in training seminars.

3. Women in development: Starting small-scale pilot projects to make women self-reliant.

PACWA also networks with Women of Global Action (WOGA), formerly called AD 2000. I was never more perplexed than one day in 1990 when Luis Bush, president of AD 2000, called me. It had been a tiresome day, and I almost ignored the call. The name Bush and title "president" in his introduction caused me to confuse him with the American president,

George Bush. He had called to inform me that, after much prayer and consulting with the Lord, they felt they should request me to serve as the chairperson of the women's track of the AD 2000 convention. At the end of the millennium, the AD 2000 women's track merged with Global Action's women's track, WOGA. This has brought great transformation to Africa through the support of Lars Dunberg and Emily Vowhein, leaders of Global Action. In addition to prayer and much-needed financial and material support, they also send short-term missionaries to Africa to run children's camps in the slums.

CONCLUSION

If it were not for these four men, my life probably would have been very different. I can not imagine how rough and tough things would be without my husband's tangible support and love. I can not overstate the efforts of my late father to raise me up as a daughter of purpose, which God has continually unfolded in my life. My pastors have offered invaluable advice, prayer, and encouragement, and I hold them in high esteem: Pastor White (who has since returned to Canada) and Dr. Adeyemo. I have seen the value of working together in harmony—it brings glory to God. It is important to take up our rightful positions in God and to let the will of God our Father be done.

Looking back, I see God's intervention in the women's ministry that he calls his own. I appreciate Dr. Adeyemo, who was there to encourage, pray for, and counsel me in those times of feeling inadequate to take up the responsibility at PACWA, and for the key role he prayed in the incorporation of AD 2000's women's track in PACWA.

What could I have done without you gentlemen? For those who are still alive, thank God with me. For my dad who has gone to glory, he has received a better reward. To all of you, I say thank you. I am what I am because you allowed God to touch me through you. Amen.

4

Under the Mango Tree: A Missionary's Story

Nancy Hudson

WHEN I WAS FIRST asked to write something about the men who had an effect on my life and ministry, I had to search my mind and heart. It all began with Jesus, my master and friend and truly my hero. He was always there patiently waiting for me as I lived my life, raising my three children alone and thinking I was "okay." I was not.

Jesus really began to deal with me about a year before I actually was saved. I was a career woman with a good job, living my life, loving my kids, being worldly in some respects, but having the benefit of a Christian sister who was always praying for me. I would tell her not to push religion at me. One night, as I was dozing off to sleep, the room lit up from an outside light. Many people, all dressed in white, were rising up into the air with arms raised. It scared me a lot. When my sister visited me the next day, I told her what had happened, saying it was like a dream, but I was not sleeping. She explained that I had a vision of the "rapture." I did not have a clue what she was talking about. She showed me a passage in the Bible describing exactly what I saw: "for the Lord Himself will descend from heaven with a shout, with the voice of the archangel and with the trumpet of God, and the dead in Christ will rise first. Then we who are alive and remain will be caught up together with them in the clouds to meet the Lord in the air, and so we shall always be with the Lord" (1 Thess 4:16–17 NASB). Wow! But I was still scared. The earthly human being truly does not comprehend things of the Spirit.

PASTOR GENO DEMARCO

In 1981, I began to receive many witnesses in my life: people sharing papers, or "religious literature," as I called them—a real drawing from God, for which I will be eternally grateful. I then was invited to an "outreach" event by a friend. People were worshipping and singing praise songs so joyfully that I really became caught up in it. It was then that I noticed the drummer, a man whom I knew from high school some twenty-five years before. I asked my friend about him. His name was Eugene DeMarco, called Geno by friends who knew him years back as a high school football player who was always full of joy and good humor. My friend then told me that he was now a pastor of a church in my hometown of New Brighton, Pennsylvania. I was so amazed that I had to smile, still not understanding the things of the Spirit. He then preached a message from the Bible.

Later, my sister came to visit me, and I took her to this "outreach." She was delighted that the Lord had put me right in the midst of a community of faith, just as she had prayed. I told her about Geno DeMarco, whom she also knew from high school. A few weeks later, I felt led to attend the church where he pastored. My daughter, Debbie, who was nineteen at the time, attended with me. His anointed preaching led her and me to the altar together, where we gave our hearts to the Lord. Needless to say, he recognized me and was as surprised to see me up there as I had been to see him. My life changed! I sat under his ministry for three years, learning and driving him crazy with hundreds of questions at all hours of the day and night. He was so patient and taught me so much. His example to me as a man of God inspired me to move forward in my Christian life and never turn back. He is a man of faith and truth who never compromised what he believed in. During this time, my son Robert, who was sixteen, also went forward in a service and gave his heart to the Lord. A few months later, my other son, Rick, who was eighteen and in the United States Navy, came home on leave and went to the church with me, and he too went forward to be saved.

Pastor DeMarco was so touched by this that he stood up at the altar with him and wept for joy, and told the congregation that now my whole family had given their lives to the Lord. Though I was a new Christian, Pastor DeMarco trusted me enough to go on hospital visitation and sent me out on evangelism with teams. Many people were being saved and coming to the church. After three years, I began to feel a need to learn more about missions. He encouraged me, had me appointed to the mission board at church, and taught me. I was always interested in the missionaries who would visit the church. The organization with which my church was affiliated, the International Fellowship of Christian Assemblies (IFCA), had a mini mission program in which teams would form to go to a different country or countries each year. I "happened" to be given a brochure about the team going that year to Barbados. I lit up and I knew I had to go. Pastor Geno encouraged me greatly and appealed for the funds that I needed. I remember needing $960 for the trip, and in the offerings during the month, a total of $961 came in! This was a clear indication of God's call, and I went on that mission trip with much joy! It was there that I received the "mission call." I stood in that country, looking at the poor people, physically and spiritually, and my burden for souls became so big and material things became so small as the call got stronger. I knew I had to go, but I felt so inadequate.

PASTOR DAN MORRELL

Enter Pastor Dan Morrell, the leader of the team to Barbados. Pastor Dan had been a missionary in Barbados for eight years and was leading the team to the area where his church and friends were. He was the next hero to boost me into the missions call. The members of that team were equipped to carry out different ministries, such as programs for children, youth, mothers, etc. I did not feel like I could do anything worthwhile. This is where Pastor Dan found me: all alone in my room crying and feeling sorry for myself. From that moment on, we became the best of friends. He was so full of missions knowledge, and he taught me much about cross-cultural ministry: other people groups, world missions, different countries, persecutions, and the prayer needs of other nations. I will be forever grateful to him. It was he who brought out my gift of evangelism. Missionary, yes, but also evangelist! Personal evangelism was my calling. He discovered it while observing that I would go up to anyone, including Rastafarians in Barbados, and lead them to Jesus. Pastor Dan and I are still best friends after twenty-five years. He has visited me in South Africa several times and still helps when I have a question or problem about missions. He actually led the first mini mission team of twelve to South Africa to visit me in 1992.

Now back to Pastor DeMarco. When the call came to me in Barbados to be a missionary, I came back to my church and shared the news with my pastor. He immediately, and without question, knew that I had heard from God. He has always been my encourager when problems came our way. He made many calls seeking mission work for me, but to no avail. My organization had no openings for a single, middle-aged woman, and I was trying every mission organization there was. I was rejected by all of them for various reasons: because I was too old, I was single, I did not have a college degree, I did not have formal Bible training, I did not have any talent or gifting. I would sob in despair with every rejection, as I wanted to go so badly and tell the world about Jesus. Someone said that I had to have a burden for a particular country. I did not. I just wanted to go where God wanted me. I was willing to go anywhere. My pastor would cry with me, and pray and pray. One day, I received a call from the headquarters of my organization asking me to come the next day to the office and meet a man who was a mission leader with Operation Mobilization. He was the director of a missionary ship called the M. V. Logos.

REV. FRANK FORTUNATO

When I met the director, Rev. Frank Fortunato, he just sat and listened to me speak from my heart. When I was finished, he said, as if he had heard from God, "You have a missionary heart. Would you like to come and join me on the ship Logos for three months and learn more about missions firsthand?" Wow! I had pictured myself tramping through jungles or something, and not on a ship, of all things. Therefore, I told him I would pray and get back to him the next day. I went home and opened my Bible right to Revelation 3:8: "I know your deeds. See, I have placed before you an open door that no one can shut . . ." (TNIV). I knew that it was of God, and I had to go. I phoned Frank the next morning, and he set up orientation for me at their headquarters, which was just beginning that following week.

I left for the mission ship Logos in August 1985, meeting it in Belize, Central America. Brother Frank met me when I arrived and introduced me to the rest of the crew. Most of the people on the ship were young people in discipleship training. They were having a welcome ceremony with dignitaries of the town there. I could not tell the difference between the dignitaries and the ship personnel, but I felt completely at home. It was not long before I became the ship "mother" and evangelist, working in the book exhibition on the ship. The ship Logos sold educational and Christian books, going from country to country and evangelizing along the way. My God fulfilled a dream to go into all the world and share the gospel with everyone (Mark 16:15). My three-month invitation turned into two years, and the best two years of my life, going from country to country, meeting missionaries, and experiencing other cultures as we went to many nations in Central and South America. The ship personnel, who were mostly young people, were missionaries from forty different countries. What a privilege to be there! I will be forever grateful to Frank Fortunato, who heard from God and invited me when no one else wanted me. We are still friends after twenty-six years. He, too, eventually visited me in South Africa, and we had the privilege of working together on a trip to India in 2006.

JOHN HUDSON

During my time on the ship Logos, I met an English man named John Hudson. He was to become my husband, the last thing on earth that I was thinking about. God had ordained it all from the very beginning. John and I began a friendship on the ship. He didn't like me too much at first, as I was more outgoing, an American, and Pentecostal. He was very shy, not too outgoing, never married, not very confident, from English culture, an Anglican, and a bit younger than I. I respected his love for the Lord, his heart for missions, and his burden for souls, which showed during evangelism outreach when he, in spite of his shyness, would share Jesus with others. As our friendship grew, we came to like each other, and we began to understand each other more. There was a policy on the ship that there were to be no relationships on board between men and women without the approval of the ship leadership. This was the social policy called "SP," or "special permission." A man would have to go to leadership and ask permission to have courtship with a girl, and then she would have to agree. Well, when I was approached about this, I was never so embarrassed and flattered at the same time in my whole life. The ship leadership was reluctant to grant us permission because of the many differences in our lives, so we were "secret" for a few months until we prayed more about it. We then decided it was from God and wanted the permission. So, then the leaders decided we should take the matter to our pastors. I had to write to Pastor DeMarco about this possible relationship, and he, with a smile to his wife, Norma, said, "Why not? I know Nancy would not be doing anything that the Lord would not ordain." And so, after completing our ship duty, we returned to the States and were married. My church gave us a beautiful wedding. We then visited England for a short while and met his church family and friends and his immediate family before returning to the United States. My pastor and church embraced John and put us to work in the church teaching evangelism and doing visitation. We began seeking mission work again as we both desired to go back to the field. We met with opposition for the same reasons for which I had been rejected previously. Nevertheless, my pastor met an evangelist who knew about a mission in South Africa that needed help. Through these contacts, we found ourselves on the way to a new life in April of 1989.

We arrived in South Africa with only two suitcases, and we did not know anyone. We knew nothing of the apartheid in effect at that time—the legal separation of the Black and White people. We began our work with the help of a couple who had a mission center, and it was there that we learned much about the culture and country. We also saw the mistreatment of the Black people, which we just did not understand. We had such a desire to go into the villages and minister to the Black people, but we were told we could not go. It was dangerous, we could get disease, we needed permits, and we were not wanted there. The more we insisted on going there, the more we were mistreated. We were continually in contact with Pastor DeMarco about the situation, and trusting us, he advised us to go out on our own.

A certain White woman named Sally had befriended us and, through her, the Lord opened doors: a place to live, fellowship with other Christians, and ministry among the workers at her farm. We did then go into the villages with a local pastor who translated for us, and we began to see a strong movement of God as the people would listen to us. They were amazed that White people would come to their homes. Because of the love of Jesus, many were being saved. We were led to a very poor squatter camp of Mozambican refugees. The war in Mozambique at that time was driving these people through the Kruger Animal Park, and we heard horrifying stories of refugees being eaten by lions or killed by Cape buffalo. Many of the refugees were being saved, accepting Jesus as their Savior, and beginning a new way of life. Some of the refugees were working on the farm of my friend. As time went on in South Africa, we planted two churches in the villages where some of these refugees settled. We returned to the United States after the first year to share our experiences with our church and to gain support to return to South Africa, as we knew that was where God was leading us. We returned to South Africa in September of 1990 to continue the task God put before us. My friend on the farm built us a small cottage where we stayed for five years. We ended up in a village called Moshakga where we planted our first church under a mango tree. We would go door to door, have open-air meetings under the tree, and then started building a wooden plank church.

During one of these door-to-door ministries, I visited a certain family and shared the gospel. The older brother in the family living there, named Jonas Mangena, hated White people because of the oppression and wondered why I would even be there. He saw me showing love to his family, and being curious, he began following me around. He saw Jesus in our actions and eventually came to the mango tree and was saved. This young man was eighteen years old at the time, and I have since watched him grow into a powerful man of God. He was to become another one of my heroes. As I watched John disciple Jonas and other young men, I began to realize how God was changing him also. From a shy man, he was becoming a powerful preacher and worship leader. He taught others to play the guitar and learn new English songs, as he himself would learn the native language Sotho songs, which the people loved. We moved to a house nearer to the village where we worked and began to build a brick church at Moshakga. Many of the people who were part of that church became leaders in the future. I would teach Sunday school, minister to children and youth, and train other teachers. John would teach the word and lead music. John became sick in 1996, and we went back to the United States in February of 1997 so he could begin treatment for lymphoma. He passed away in August of 1997. I know the Lord welcomed him as his good and faithful servant. He truly was!

JONAS MANGENA

I knew my calling, and had to return to South Africa, where I am today. All of the people accepted me back with open arms and named me to be their pastor and continue the work. During this time, there were vast political changes in South Africa as a Black government was elected and apartheid ended. Freedom had come to South Africa, and we began to see prosperity come to the country and to the Black people. Pastor Jonas became my assistant, and then my associate and general overseer of the ministry we call CASA (Christian Assemblies of South Africa). We planted eight more churches and trained the pastors for each one. Jonas married a young woman named Agnes who had been my assistant and translator. He now has three children and is very active in the ministry. He has been by my side consistently, helping me with every aspect of the ministry, from training leaders and planting and building churches to teaching and preaching. He is one of the most powerful worship leaders in our area. All that has been accomplished in South Africa could not have happened without him by my side, encouraging me, loving me, always ready to do anything asked of him. He is the oldest of a family of ten, all of whom are committed to or active in the ministry, including the mother and father. One brother, Phillip, is a pastor, another sister, Jeaneth, has gone to Malawi to be a missionary. The others are in music ministry and teaching. Jonas has helped train them all and helps me with everything, always by my side. I always call him my hero. It has been eighteen years since I met him, and he is still faithful, totally committed to the things of God, to me, and to the goals that I set for the ministry. God had a plan, and when it is his plan, no one can stop it.

I am forever grateful to the Lord for putting these men in my life to help me fulfill the calling that God put on my heart. I can only give him the glory for it all! In my Christian life, and especially as a ministry leader and a missionary, I have seen men try to stop women from going into ministry. I am an example. I would say that, when God has a plan, no one can stop it. I would encourage men today to look at the potential for enlarging God's kingdom through powerful women of God and to accept them as partners in ministry, as we will be forever worshipping the Lord side by side. Females have God-given talents, knowledge, and wisdom for use in his kingdom. Barriers have been set in place by tradition, rituals, and doctrines that have been misused or that have taken the word and distorted it, hindering women from moving into the places where God wants them. God sees neither male nor female. God's call is upon a life for service, without regard to gender.

Men's ministries have been enlarged by faithful women members and those called into ministry in the local churches and elsewhere. Pastor Geno DeMarco, with his kind, understanding, no-nonsense ways, lifted me up into ministry the same way that Jesus taught and mentored his disciples. Pastor Geno mentored me and encouraged me to move into my call-ing. Notice what happened when a committed man of God did this! Pastor Dan Morrell's passion for missions caught my heart and made me desire to learn all I could about missions, which has benefited me for twenty-six years. Rev. Frank Fortunate "heard" from God. I learned that, when you listen carefully, God will clearly reveal to anyone what he wants done. Frank is now the international music director for Operation Mobilization. He travels worldwide teaching music, especially in areas where the persecuted church is located. Frank taught me to listen. Pastor John Hudson, who was exemplary in his perseverance in overcoming low self-esteem and his pas-sion for souls and for music, taught me that, even with a lack of confidence, God will move in and make a difference in your life when you allow him to. Pastor Jonas Mangena, a real student of the word, is strongly committed to God. I am eternally grateful that the Lord took him out of the world of darkness and brought him into the light. His submission to the will of God allowed him to submit to me as his pastor. And, at the same time, I drew from his strength of conviction and his knowledge of the land, the people, and the customs of South Africa that enables me to be more successful in the ministry to which God called me.

South Africa was a very male-dominated country where women were in submission to men, under subjection all the time, and mistreated emotionally as well as physically. Times have changed now, and women have more rights. But, in the time of oppression, the church men accepted me as their pastor and the villagers saw and agreed. I believe this was a God-given gift so that other women could be called into the ministry without problems. We now have another woman pastor in the ministry and several women leading ministries within our organization of CASA. Yes, strong Christian men can give priceless support to women in min-istry to help them become all that God wants them to be. These men are the heroes to me.

5

Who I Am: A Racing Car Driver Becomes a Globetrotting Professor

Gwendolyn Joy Dewey

I AM GWEN, A child of God, married to my childhood sweetheart, Don, mother of three wonderful daughters, Kim, Kelly, and Kacey. Over my lifetime, I have been many things: farmer, high school teacher, counselor, school administrator, college professor, airplane pilot, financial advisor, researcher, international traveler, and founding president of a university, to name a few. For much of my early adult life, I was a student. I have a bachelor of science degree in psychology, a master's in educational psychology, and a doctorate in educational policy, governance, and administration, all from the University of Washington. I also have a doctor of ministry degree in transformational leadership from Eastern Baptist School of Theology. Not satisfied with all this, I also took master's-level courses in theology at Fuller Theological Seminary, took training for a Series 6 brokerage license, took classes and training to become a licensed pilot, learned to drive race cars, and took classes in welding for art. I am essentially a learning junkie.

MY MINISTRY INVOLVEMENT

Today, true to my passion for learning, I am teaching seminary students, other professors, pastors, church leaders, and businesspeople around the world about the theology of work (TOW). I also am the director of doctoral dissertations at Bakke Graduate University (BGU), located in

Seattle, Washington. This university of more than five hundred students in masters and doctoral programs looks beyond itself to embrace a global network of urban leaders, partners, and alumni for individual, organizational, and community transformation.

MY STORY

How I got to where I am now is convoluted, as are most life stories. However, it is clear that my heavenly Father, always with me, was graciously guiding me. My unique childhood days growing up in Richland, Washington, God's gracious and forgiving love, and a few great Christian men who came into my life and supported and influenced me are by far the primary influencing agents in my life.

During the Great Depression years of the 1930s, my parents, prior to their marriage in 1937, lived in the Arkansas Ozarks. People from the Ozarks have been referred to as "hillbillies" because of their location in the "hills and hollers" of the Ozark Mountains and their isolated and independent lifestyle of living solely off the land. However, my newly married parents broke away from this and followed a mass migration happening at that time going from Arkansas to California to find work. This great exodus of people in search of jobs is recorded in John Steinbeck's famous novel *Grapes of Wrath*, published in 1939. Never during my mother's lifetime could she read Steinbeck's novel. It brought back too many painful memories.

My father found work as a truck driver and my parents lived in temporary tent housing in Salinas, California, which was provided by farm owners for the many migrant workers. Not long after I was born in 1938, my father heard that unionized truck drivers were being paid twice his salary in Neosho, Missouri, and our family moved there. Then, in 1942, we followed another large migration of Arkansas and Oklahoma workers to work on a top-secret facility being constructed in Richland, Washington. We did not know it at the time, but it was the government's Manhattan Project, the place where plutonium would be manufactured to make one of the two first atomic bombs.

Richland, up to 1942, was a very small town of 247 people. Richland is located where the Columbia, Snake, and Yakima Rivers join together. The United States government chose Richland as the production site for the very secret Manhattan Project, which to us was called the Hanford Project, because of its abundant water for cooling the atomic reactor piles, its isolation (nothing but desert), and ease of restricting access to protect from sabotage. In a very short time, this small town was transformed into a federally owned town of 11,000 people. It became a place where scientists and laborers worked and lived side by side. Only families who worked on the Hanford Project and had security clearances were allowed to live in Richland and rent these government-owned homes. If one were to lose his or her job, he or she had to move out immediately.

The type of house one could rent was based on the status and pay of the employee. Alphabet letters were used to identify the type of house: A, B, C, F, G, H, etc. Streets were named after scientists, national leaders, and trees. There were a few large homes located by the Columbia River for the scientists, but the bulk of the workers were housed in much smaller prefabricated houses. These houses went up in a very short time. Each one could be built by a few workers in less than one week. Every person working at the Hanford Project was considered important to its success, and each worker felt needed and valued. This concept of equality based on each person's role in the goal of the Hanford Project stayed with me throughout my life.

One thing was certain: The education one had determined social standing within the town. Scientific education was the most highly regarded profession, but other post-college degrees followed close behind. At the bottom, where the vast majority of the people were located, were those with no advanced education at all. Education equaled success, honor, good job, respect, and money. Since the town was completely federally operated, the schools were superb. This emphasis on education had a large impact on my graduating class of 358 students in 1956: A large percentage continued in post–high school education, and about one-fifth of these ended up with doctoral degrees.

My father, whom I care for, is now ninety-five years old. He was never out of work and always provided for his family. He loved me and treated me very specially as the firstborn of four children. Although his grandfather had been a traveling Baptist minister, riding on horseback to various communities in northwestern Arkansas, he never went to church with us, as he worked different shifts and almost never had Sunday off. He left it to my mother to take us to church.

Churches had not yet been constructed, and church attendees met in school buildings. My mother took me with her to a newly formed Assembly of God congregation, and I continued attending this church, which later built a church building, all the way through my school years in Richland. When I was six years old, I made a commitment to follow Christ as my Lord. I became actively involved in the Saturday morning Children's Church, Sunday morning and evening services, Wednesday night prayer meeting service, and Friday night young people's service. Wes Banta, my first pastor, had a love and a heart for engaging young people in the church. He often took about thirty of us young people, nine to fifteen years of age, on trips to other churches to show what we could do. I was the youngest of the group. My job was to recite verses from memory and quote all the names of the books of the Bible. Some of the other kids quoted large portions of Scripture, played musical instruments, and sang in duets, trios, and quartets, and then we all sang together. Every summer we went to a Christian summer camp for a week—one week for girls and one week for boys—on Deer Lake located near Spokane, Washington. I loved my church and all the activities in which I was engaged.

I excelled at school and was always at the top of my classes. I loved learning and strived for excellence in everything I did. I fully believed higher education in a scientific field was the path to success.

Our congregation built a church not far from the junior and senior high schools I attended. By then we had a new pastor, Rev. Walter Buck, who later performed the marriage ceremony for my husband and me after I graduated from high school. Rev. Buck also loved young people and set up a short service every Monday morning before school to inspire us to live Christian lives at school and to excel in all we did.

As I grew older, however, I became disenchanted by the behavior and level of interest of the other kids in the church. They seemed to live in a different world than mine. They were in a closed church world, one which excluded the school world. I tried to merge the two worlds together, but I could not do it. I became embarrassed by their lack of interest in school, so I began to separate myself from them. Many of my church friends thought it was sinful for me to ever think about going to college when I graduated. They felt that everyone who wanted to do post–high school study should go to a Bible school. However, my drive for higher education was strong and geared toward studying a scientific field. Nothing was going to stop me. I gradually grew less interested in the church. Later, it fell back on my husband, Don, to bring me back to walking with God.

DON DEWEY, MY LIFELONG FRIEND AND HUSBAND

Don and I have known each other since I was six years old. I believe Don is the most influential man in my life. Along with God's loving grace, Don's prayers and influence on me are the reason I am a Christian today and actively working in ministry. Don and I grew up in the same unique city and environment and went to the same church. Unlike many of the other church kids, Don went to college. When he was a senior at Washington State University and I had graduated from high school, we married. I immediately started college, and in between the births of three children, I was able to complete my bachelor of science degree in psychology with a teaching certificate in English and psychology by age thirty. Don and I fully partnered in everything we did, including the family chores, cooking, and parenting and childcare.

After Don graduated from college in electrical engineering, we moved many times, going from the West Coast to the East Coast. With all these moves, we eventually stopped going regularly to church. After settling down in Seattle, Don nudged us back into a church where we would be sure to find solid teaching and one that honored and respected businesspeople. We found a wonderful Lutheran pastor who was a great teacher, and we attended his extended Bible courses, which were taught in a scholarly way. We were now attending church on a regular basis.

Don kept reading, studying, and growing in his biblical understanding as his faith became renewed. We bought a raspberry farm in Puyallup, Washington, where we wanted to raise our daughters. We began attending a Swedish Baptist church. Don alternately taught the college-age and adult classes in the Sunday school program and occasionally played the piano and organ for our church services.

Meanwhile, my career had taken off and my life became filled with continuing education, finishing my master's and then my doctorate degree, enjoying my family, running our raspberry farm during the summer picking time, and traveling with Don and our family around the world on vacations and to Don's many NATO meetings. Don's parents stayed with us much of this time, and my mother was close by, so we had an extended family on our farm.

Then, I began to drift and I became a Sunday worshipper. I did not have a musical talent, I didn't have time to volunteer for tending the nursery or making cookies or food to be sent to shut-ins; in short, I didn't think I had anything to contribute within the walls of the church. My church had no theology for recognizing that God calls people to serve outside of the walls of the church in their workplaces as well as within the church. Don and I were fully aware of our differences, so, after being unable to resolve them, he took a new tack: pray (daily) for me and leave it up to God. This lasted for many years.

Later, a better understanding of the theology of work made me realize that during this time I was in ministry doing the will of God, which is what he had prepared for me to do. My calling was to education. I had never been taught that God cares about schools, children, and the educational process in the community, and that he places us there to serve as salt and light and serve the people he created.

In the early 1990s, Don told Lowell Bakke, our new pastor at the time, that he would give anything for me to find joy in a walk with God. Only later, after having a better understanding of the Christian faith as provided by Lowell, Ray, and Dennis Bakke, did I understand how to merge the two worlds. When I did get on my path of discovery, Don did something unique: He retired from his rewarding and prestigious career and began to help me prepare for a new career. He filled in much-needed context and background information as well as guiding my studies. Many husbands simply do not go the distance that Don did.

I was now beginning to really learn, but it took three Bakke brothers to lead me through a ten-year journey of discovery.

DR. LOWELL BAKKE

Lowell Bakke opened up the first door that led me out of the closed church and into the community. Our church of nearly five hundred began shrinking and dying after our pastor left. There were several interim pastors, but when it shrank to fewer than one hundred, Lowell was called to help this little old dying church. I had no idea that my life would be turned upside down. Soon, I learned that everything I knew, had experienced, and had done was fully God's kingdom work. But even more astounding, God had already been using me in kingdom work, and I didn't even know it.

When Lowell came to the church, my faith was renewed. Lowell visited us in our home and visited me in my workplace in the school district where I was one of the top administrators. He never talked "church" to me. He just talked with me to find out about the school district, my interests, and my knowledge of our city. He wanted to engage the school district and get to know how our church, Bethany, could serve the city and the schools. Lowell wanted to find out where the heart of the city was, and he discovered that the football stadium was the sanctuary of Puyallup. The entire Puyallup community gathered around the stadium, where their children played sports, marched in bands, played in orchestras, and sang in choral groups. Lowell was the first pastor who opened my eyes to the role of the church outside its walls, and showed me that we all have a mandate to serve where we live and work.

Lowell told me that my role with the school district, my calling as an educator, was ministry. He expanded on how God places each of us as salt and light to serve God. I began to feel included. Teaching a Sunday school class or tending the nursery at church was not the only way one could be in ministry. I began to engage in church, and I felt I was making a contribution.

Lowell's gift is coaching. He walked with me and showed me places where God was already working. He took a small group of us from Bethany to a Visions of Hope for the City conference in New York City to see how God was working in urban areas. While there, we met his brother, Dr. Raymond Bakke, who had been called by *Christianity Today* the "the Apostle to the City."[1] Ray was leading a group of doctor of ministry students from Eastern Baptist Theological Seminary in a class designed to view a wide variety of ministries in New York City and see models of ministry that were transforming the city for the kingdom. I became excited as I began to see how my preparation in the field of education, my love for working with men and women in all ethnic groups, my innate curiosity about how systems and the world worked, and my love for learning might be able to be used for kingdom ministry in a new way.

When we returned from New York, Lowell brought a Christian resource ministry team to Bethany to conduct a three-weekend seminar. We mapped out how the events and people in our past had shaped us, discussed our interests, gifts, and talents, and talked about how God might use these in preparing us for future ministry. God was definitely beginning to work with me and was preparing me for a big change.

Ray often came to our church to preach and share how God was working in cities around the world. As I heard more from Ray and about

1. Kauffman, "Apostle to the City."

the doctor of ministry program he was leading with Dr. Leah Fitchue at Eastern Baptist Theological Seminary (EBTS, now Palmer Theological Seminary), I became interested in the program and saw this as a way to learn more about how God was working globally. I wanted to participate with God in a new way.

DR. RAY BAKKE

Ray Bakke opened up the second door out of the closed church into the urban centers of the world. Ray enabled me to see how God was working through people around the world. Early in 1996, God really began to stir in me a new desire to go to seminary and to study for a doctor of ministry degree (D.Min.) in transformational leadership in the urban global world. Although I already had a doctorate from the University of Washington, I did not have a master of divinity (M.Div.) or any academic work in theology. However, feeling undaunted and with an assurance that I could do anything I set my mind to, I slipped away from home one Sunday afternoon to talk with Ray while he was visiting Lowell. I began asking questions about the D.Min. program at EBTS. When Ray informed me that he would be leaving the program at EBTS in June 2000 to retire, I became a little panicked, because I thought he had the information I was searching for. Little did I know that Ray and Lowell had been planning to get me into the EBTS D.Min. program. As we talked, a plan was hatched: I would take a set of basic theology courses in the M.Div. program at Fuller Seminary, which would enable me to be accepted into the EBTS program.

Pursuing two degrees at the same time seemed daunting at first. This new direction caused me to think of quitting my job as school administrator and even my job teaching in the Graduate School of Administration at Pacific Lutheran University. I returned home that afternoon and talked with Don, who was stunned to learn that I had the desire to study theology. Don had long been praying that I would rekindle my desire to serve and know God better, but this announcement completely floored him. "Obviously," he told me, "praying for you was the right thing to do. Telling you what to do has never worked and never will." Again, my husband, the ultimate encourager and helpmate, told me to go for it. I applied to Fuller Seminary and to EBTS at the same time, and I was accepted into both programs. My life was really going to change now.

I must admit that I was theologically in kindergarten when I took my first class on the synoptic gospels at Fuller, which was being taught by Dr. Kent Ginger, the dean of Fuller's M.Div. program. Don attended all my Fuller classes with me as an audit student. I was never afraid to ask questions, as I always told my students we learn by questioning. However, when I raised my hand the first time and asked, "What does eschatology mean?" Don slid partway under his desk, embarrassed by my almost total lack of theological knowledge. The class, and especially Dr. Ginger, enjoyed the moment. But God was gracious to me, knew I liked to learn, and sent his Holy Spirit to be alongside me and teach me. I found I loved studying the Bible! I could not seem to get enough. This was a new finding for me. God was at work.

It was at this time Ray asked Don to be the chairman of his board for international urban associates. I went with Ray and Don to Xiamen, China, for a consultation with educational and ministry leaders of the city and again saw how God was working around the world.

I loved my time studying at Fuller and EBTS. I studied in both programs at the same time and completed my D.Min. at EBTS in May, 2000. In August of 2000, Ray Bakke asked me to join him in the trans-Pacific alliance as the academic dean for a new D.Min. program in transformational leadership for the global urban city for this new coalition of three seminaries: Carey Theological Seminary in Vancouver, British Columbia; the Asian Theological Seminary in Manila; and Northwest Graduate School of the Ministry (NWGS) in Kirkland, Washington.

In January 2001, the leadership and ownership of NWGS was assumed by our small group. The trans-Pacific alliance was merged into NWGS, and a new board was formed, chaired by Dr. David McKenna, former president of Spring Harbor University, Seattle Pacific University, and Asbury Theological Seminary.

DR. DAVID MCKENNA, MY LEADERSHIP MENTOR, JUST WHEN I NEEDED IT

Dave McKenna, a nationally known guru in leadership, particularly university leadership, faithfully mentored me in fulfilling my role as president at NWGS and then as founding president of what is now Bakke Graduate University (BGU). I am greatly indebted to Dave for helping me serve as president of BGU during the "years of discovery." It was Ray's dream to work with a school that would serve the world's leaders without requiring them to leave their ministries and leadership roles to attend classes in the US, and it was Dave's willingness that helped make that dream come true. The dream included using the world's largest cities as crucibles for learning, allowing students to see where God was working in large global urban settings, and allowing our students learn directly from indigenous practitioners. Ray did not want to be the president, and he did not wish to be an administrator, because his true gift was teaching church history and urban ministry. I was asked by Ray and Dave to be the founding president of the school, and I accepted yet another challenge.

Dave had retired as the president of Asbury Theological Seminary in Wilmore, Kentucky, and moved back to the Seattle area. He had formerly served as the president of Seattle Pacific University and Spring Arbor College and was a member of the executive committee of the National Association of Evangelicals and the World Methodist Council, among many other groups. He is the author of many books on leadership.[2]

Although I had been in key leadership roles before, I clearly needed additional skills in my role as president of the school. Dave committed to spending every Monday morning for two to three hours (or more sometimes) going over any questions I had and mentoring me in the process of dealing with school boards. I grew to love him and found his advice invaluable. I could not have performed my role without his wise advice, counsel, and support. He is indeed a godly man of great wisdom who took the time to share with me and teach me many things.

I never set out to be the president of a university, but God had placed me in the right spot when someone was needed with my background, which included a doctoral degree and experience in the field of leadership and administration policies at the college level, along with a D.Min. in the subject the school would be based upon in the future. Our wonderful God and these two men, Ray and Dave, helped me birth this fledgling university. Following in the steps of Ray, and using the program he taught at EBTS, our new school uses the world's largest cities as crucibles of learning to provide students with an up-close engagement in those cities to allow them to see and study how God is working in the world. This university

---

2. Among his works are *Power to Follow, Grace to Lead,* (1989) and a later one to which I referred frequently, *Never Blink in a Hailstorm and Other Lessons on Leadership* (2005).

has miraculously grown and now has close to five hundred students from around the world studying in master's and doctoral programs.

After two years, I felt my mission was over, and the university needed a person more qualified in fundraising, contacts, and leadership skills to take it to the next level. Dr. Brad Smith became the new president. I had steered the school through the first phase of the accreditation cycle and had put the school on an academically sound basis. I remain with the school I love and serve as the director of dissertations. Now, I have had a new assignment given to me by the final Bakke brother, Dennis, who, with his brother Lowell, has the expansive vision of reaching the entire world with the theology of work.

DENNIS BAKKE

Dennis Bakke opened up the third door leading into the rest of the world for me. Dennis was raised in Saxon, Washington, born in between Ray (the oldest) and Lowell. While Ray and Lowell became pastors, he followed a different path, encouraged by his mother, Ruth. Dennis's calling was to business. Dennis achieved much in his early years, graduating from the University of Puget Sound, Harvard Business School, and the National War College. He cofounded the AES Corporation in 1981 and served as its president and CEO from 1994 to 2002. AES became the world's second largest energy producing company with 40,000 employees and $8.6 billion in revenue by 2002.

For a while, the only thing I knew about Dennis was what I had been told by Lowell and Ray and what I had read in the *Wall Street Journal*. I knew Dennis believed that, like his brothers, he was doing kingdom work. Slowly, I learned what he meant. Work, when done for God and done as God's steward, is in itself ministry. To work in partnership with God is why we were created. We experience great joy when we are doing God's work. Poring over Dennis's national bestselling book, *Joy at Work*, and Brad Smith, Ray Bakke, and William Hendricks's book, *Joy at Work Bible Study Companion*, I finally understood what it was all about. I did some additional research and found that this whole concept has been around for a long time—it was a major cornerstone of the Reformation.

So why had I not known before that all my schooling, work, and family belong to God? Why had I not heard that God made us to work and finds joy in our work if it is done in the name of the Lord Jesus (Col

3:17 TNIV), and that our work can be a means of honoring God and serving our neighbor? In Hebrew Scripture, *avodah* means "work and worship" as well as "service." Why had I not heard in the churches I had attended all these years that God wanted us to be coworkers with him, creating new and useful products and services that benefit all people? God left his created people with the ability to use their creative spirits to continue creating things like useful electricity, health services, vehicles for transportation, art, and music, to name just a few. In Genesis 2:5–8, we read that shrubs and plants had not yet sprung up because "there was no one to work the ground," and so "God formed a man from the dust of the ground and breathed into his nostrils the breath of life" (TNIV) to work and tend his creation.

In 2006, Lowell and Dennis met to discuss this very problem. What could be done to change churches around the world so they would recognize and nourish those in the workplace as ministers? They decided to do this by changing the next generation of pastors by establishing the theology of work in seminaries. They created a theology of work grant program, which was established within the Mustard Seed Foundation administered through Bakke Graduate University.

I was asked to work with Lowell Bakke to administer the theology of work (TOW) grant program to create master's and doctoral level TOW courses to be taught at seminaries. This I did by seeking out the experts who had written and taught marketplace ministry, such as R. Paul Stevens at Regent College, Vancouver; Richard Higginson at Ridley Hall, Cambridge; William Messenger at Gordon-Conwell Theological Seminary in Massachusetts; and Pete Hammond with InterVarsity Christian Fellowship. I taught the very first TOW grant–sponsored class, "Joy at Work: Business as Stewardship and Mission," to a group of African bishops at the West African Theological Seminary in Lagos, Nigeria, in January 2007. The Lord blessed this class, and it was enthusiastically accepted. In this very first class, I was able to see firsthand the power of this all-embracing theology. These seventeen bishops were leaders over some eleven million church people. They are now taking the message to all of their church members.

Since then, I have taught many TOW classes around the world. Dr. Stevens became one of the most in-demand professors on our TOW teaching team. In a little less than three years, TOW grants have made it possible for more than two hundred TOW classes and seminars to be taught to more than three thousand participants, mostly at the master's and doctoral levels.

Since that time, some three years ago, Dennis and Lowell have worked with me and have been a great source of encouragement. Dennis taught me the *Joy at Work* organizational principles and, through the theology of work grant program, opened up the world for me to share these principles with, thereby leaving with me his greatest legacy. What an honor it has been to be a part of the TOW team.

REFLECTIONS

Looking back on my life, I can easily see God's leading and involvement in every step of the way. I came out of the womb a happy child with energy, health, and certain God-given abilities. I was raised in a town where it was obvious that education made all the difference in the quality and enjoyment of life. Because of my love for learning and ability to learn, I never felt unequal. I was raised in a church that allowed men and women to serve equally, but the walls of the church strangled me. However, there were positive influences provided by the church as well: I learned about faith and the walk with Christ. My first pastors encouraged me as a child to use my head, memorize and recite Scripture, and perform in front of large groups.

The Bakke brothers opened up doors of the church and showed me the fullness of what the real church looks like. Slowly, step by step, the picture came into focus. First, Lowell showed me the community and how God was working within my world. Then came Ray, who opened up a big door, showing how God is working all over the world in urban centers. What a thrill that was! Dennis opened up the final door to the whole world of work and business, allowing me to understand and teach that all our work matters to God and, when done for the glory of God, is ministry. There it was. God's world includes everything, and it is where the church is. It is not a closed-door place, but a wide-open institution that encompasses the whole earth. The blindness is gone, and I can see.

Now I can say I love the church of Jesus Christ, even though some of the congregations have a few warts. I love to worship with all sorts of congregations because I feel very much at home in different worship settings. In fact, it is the wide diversity that brings color and meaning to me. God's kingdom is so big and wonderful. But this thought is always in my mind: The earth belongs to the Lord, and everything in it (Ps 24:1 NCV). We are not owners; we are stewards of God's creation and the creative abilities he has given to each of us.

In the parable of the talents, found in Matthew 25, we read that each of the master's servants was given a different number of talents (one, two, and five) to steward in his absence. The master rewarded each servant proportionally when they faithfully worked and invested their talents, thus multiplying what they were given, saying, "Well done, good and faithful servant! You have been faithful with a few things; I will put you in charge of many things. Come and share your master's happiness [or my word, joy]" (Matt 25:21 TNIV). But the one person who did not use his talents for God, but hid the talent, the one bag of gold, because he was afraid, was reprimanded and cast into the darkness (Matt 25:30). The message is clear: We are God's stewards and are required to steward whatever talents and abilities he has given us for God's kingdom, no matter how few or how many we have.

Yes, there were times in my life I did not know I was already in ministry. But I have learned that all I have to do is make myself available to be used by God. We have a wonderful loving Father who is always gracious, forgiving, and calling us to work for and with him. May you hear his call, recognize your talents, and be prepared to work for the Father in the kingdom of God.

I thank God for the godly men who have influenced, coached, mentored, and opened doors for me. This is not about me, but about our God who is faithful and loves us and wants us to do our best in kingdom ministry. As the psalmist says, "Not to us, Lord, not to us, but to your name be the glory, because of your love and faithfulness" (Ps 115:1 TNIV).

Since this chapter was written, my role has been expanded to include overseeing academic affairs as well as heading the business school at Bakke Graduate University—all, by the grace God, through support from amazing men in my life.

6

A Tribute to Those Who Helped Me
Find My True Calling

Elke Werner

I T IS TIME TO say goodbye again. I am on my way to Slovakia where I am scheduled to speak at a European women's conference. My husband prays with me, we hug and kiss, and I take off. During the next few days, we will talk on the phone every day until I come home. Roland prays for me, encourages me, and takes on some of my duties while I am away; just like I used to and still do when he travels.

About twenty years ago, it was mainly Roland who travelled a lot. Now, it is both of us. For the last few years, in addition to my local ministry in our church in Marburg, and to my speaking ministry all over Germany, I now also work with the international Lausanne Movement as senior associate for women in evangelism. This role brings me to new places all the time, and I deeply enjoy it. Through the Lausanne network, I now minister to women all over the world. It is my desire to encourage them to be or to become who God has made and called them to be. But let me start a few years back and tell you how my husband has greatly influenced and encouraged me in my ministry.

ROOTS

I grew up in a nominal Christian home. My parents went to church on Christmas. Every week, I was sent to a children's Sunday school in our mainstream Reformed church—and I really loved it! When I was fourteen years old, my pastor asked me whether I would be willing to help in Sunday school, and I did. I just loved it. After two years, many of the older leaders retired and I started to lead the Sunday school with about one hundred kids in attendance. My pastor invited me and my small team of helpers—all teenagers—every week for a Bible study of the text we were going to present to the children on the next Sunday. That was very good training for all my work with the Bible that I am involved in nowadays. This local pastor gave me a good theological background and helped me to understand the Bible. I am still amazed at the fact that he allowed me to lead the children when I was still so young and untrained.

When I was seventeen, I first met my husband, Roland. When he was fourteen, he had started a youth group in the neighboring parish church. The youth group grew rapidly. It was the time of the Jesus-people movement. We were all young and on fire for Jesus. Teenage girls and boys preached, taught, led children's groups, evangelized on the streets, and shared the leadership of the group together. Soon there were more than 120 young people who met every Saturday afternoon. I was in the middle of it all: I preached, I taught, I led the group. Roland spent a year in the United States at that time as an exchange student. As our youth work grew, we started to invest our time and energy into children's ministry. I was responsible for four small evangelistic children's groups that met every week.

The leader of the YMCA in our town, Uwe, saw what I was doing and invited me to become a member on the board of the YMCA in our town. The YMCA in Germany is more than just sports or a health club. It is the largest evangelistic endeavor among youth in our country. After some time, I was entrusted with the responsibility of giving leadership to all the girl's groups in Duisburg, the town where I grew up. I was eighteen at that time and was the first woman they ever had on the board or in that position. It was wonderful to see how those older Christian brothers were ready to accept the leadership gifts of a young girl. For me, it was the first time to be on a board, and I learned a lot about leadership from these men. One thing I also learned was to laugh with them whenever they made jokes about the fact that I, as a young woman, was now in their group, in what used to be just a boys' club. I felt that they liked having me around even though they needed time to accept the fact that they were no longer by themselves.

LEARNING FROM THE BRETHREN

I started studying at the university and became a teacher for Christian religion and fine arts. During that time, I met wonderful older Christians from the Brethren Church who were able to teach me so much about the Bible. I accepted everything they told me because I saw their deep love for Jesus and their willingness to follow every iota of the Bible. Their attitude was exactly what I wanted, too: to be faithful to Jesus and his word. That is what I wanted, even if it meant to lay aside my leadership gifts, I was willing not to lead, not to teach, and not to preach in order to obey God's commands as they were explained to me.

For some time, I followed their example. Roland, who studied theology at that time, did not agree with my new way of looking at my role as a woman. I have always been more of a radical kind of person, and what I understood at that time was that I should be in total submission to any man who happened to be present in the same room with me. So, whenever I was leading a meeting and a boy came in, I would hand over the leadership to him, even if I knew that this might end up in chaos. The reason was just that I wanted to obey God in all respects. But Roland tried to help me understand the Bible in a different way and kept challenging me to look at the Bible verses again and see how they were meant by Paul and others. But I was not listening because I had decided that I was not going to make any compromises!

After some time, I finished my studies in Duisburg and joined Roland in Marburg, where he had gone to study Semitic languages and theology, and we got engaged. Together with friends, we started a lifelong committed community, which now has the name "Jesus-Gemeinschaft" (Fellowship of Jesus). Around that group of committed Christians grew an evangelistic group and eventually a church community in this historic university town, in which many young people came to know the Lord. Again, I was involved in many aspects of the evolving ministry: I taught, counseled, preached, led meetings, and used a variety of my spiritual gifts. But oftentimes, I did so with a troubled conscience because I was still influenced by the Brethren's view of the role of women in the church.

DISCOVERING NEW REALITIES

Roland encouraged me and all other women in our small student church to use our spiritual gifts and not to hold back using what God had entrusted to us. In 1984, I opened a Christian bookshop right in the center of our town, which is still running today. It was a challenge to lead such an endeavor. God provided all that we needed, and I slowly realized that the reality was that God had given me particular leadership gifts. This realization was stronger than my still-held theological conviction that I, as a woman, ought not to lead in the church because of my gender. I started to read many books on women in ministry, and I studied commentaries and church history. At that time, I tried the best I could to use my gifts and still submit to men. At the same time, I kept thinking that it was not fair of God to expect me to live a life with so many opportunities and challenges and still to be hindered from using my gifts.

Only when I came across books in English that were not yet translated and published in Germany did I find clear biblical analysis and alternative interpretations of the difficult verses in the Bible. I realized that maybe it was wrong to refrain from using my gifts or trying to limit my scope of ministry. In that process of reevaluation, the material produced by the group Christians for Biblical Equality was very helpful. I devoured these books and articles and found good biblical teaching and a sound theology for women in ministry. What I read here helped me to understand God and his purposes better. I found a way to interpret the Bible that made complete sense to me, did not contradict itself, and was not in conflict with the realities of my life.

Together with Roland, I studied the difficult verses again, and he was able to convince me that, in order to be true to the Bible, I had to use my gifts and see myself as a redeemed woman, a woman whom God uses with all the gifts he has given her. Roland has always been a source of sound biblical teaching to me. He studied theology, has read the Bible many times, and is totally in favor of men and women working together in true partnership and in mutual submission. If it were not for him, it would be very possible that still today I would just be a visitor in church and not an active member.

A TIME OF CRISIS

In the fall of 1988, I was diagnosed with Hodgkin disease, a cancer of the lymph system. It was detected in its last stage, and the doctors told us that I might live three more months, maybe half a year. During the year of chemotherapy, I was invited to be part of the German delegation to the second Lausanne Congress in Manila in August 1989. This invitation was very exciting to me, and also felt like a promise of God that I would still be alive in the coming summer. The invitation was even more exciting to me as, at that time, hardly anybody in Germany knew me. Roland was already a well-known author and evangelist, but I had spent most of my time working only in our local church and giving leadership on a smaller scale. So, at this point in my life, when I was extremely ill and weak, I was invited to be one of the few German female delegates for the Lausanne International Congress on World Evangelization in Manila.

When I arrived there, I was still in the middle of my chemotherapy. If I had cut myself at that time, it would have been very difficult to stop the bleeding. But I knew I had to go, and so I went. There in Manila, I witnessed a model of men and women working together on stage. Women led meetings, women were speakers, women gave testimonies, women prayed, and women led the communion service, all in partnership with men! From that time on, I knew that it is possible to be faithful to God and his word and to be in full equality with men in the use of the gifts that God has given us. What an encouragement this was to me. My whole involvement with the Lausanne Movement until today stems from this experience in Manila. The Lausanne II Congress really turned my thinking upside down.

GROWING RESPONSIBILITIES

Christian leaders in the country saw what I was doing in Marburg, and I received invitations to work with them on a broader scale. I was invited to be on the board of a mission to the Middle East. I had spent some time as an intern in Egypt, and after that, they asked me if I would be willing to be on their board. Roland's work as a linguist and Bible translator brings us to North Africa for a few weeks every year. I learned a lot about women in the Muslim world by sitting with them in their kitchens and talking to them.

In 1992, shortly after the reunification of Germany, I worked as the team leader on a cruise ship that went down the Elbe River from Dresden to Hamburg, thereby crossing the former Iron Curtain. The ship carried an exhibition on the Bible, and thousands of high school students and teachers in cities belonging to what used to be the communist eastern part of Germany came onboard to see it. Afterward, I was invited to be on the board of a coalition of about sixty evangelical mission agencies in

Germany, including Campus for Christ, the Navigators, Word of Life, and many others. Through that coalition, I started to invite women leaders to annual retreats for women who work in their respective organizations. Through these conferences, which are still ongoing and always over-booked, we as a team try to encourage them in their leadership roles.

During this time, Wilhelm, a leader in a large Christian organization, met me at one of our annual gatherings. He immediately asked me if I would be willing to come and speak at their youth gathering. I agreed. Soon after that, we received a phone call. I was in the kitchen, Roland was on the phone, and during the call he asked me, "Would you be willing to give a seminar?" My question: "How many people will be there?" "A few hundred." "And how many seminars?" "About ten." In my mind, I used these figures to calculate how many participants would possibly come to my seminar. The result was eight hundred people, ten seminars, sixty to eighty in each seminar. That would be okay for me, so I agreed. When we arrived, I was told that they had given me the big hall for my seminar. About one thousand young Christians wanted to come and hear what I had to say. If I had known that earlier, I would have said, "No way!" I would have been afraid to speak to such a large group. But I am still thankful to this Christian leader who was willing to let me speak there. A few years later, Wilhelm died and went to be with the Lord. I am thankful that back then he saw something in me that I did not see yet: the call to speak to large groups of people. It all went well, although my knees were shaking. Ever since this experience, I trust the leading hand of the Lord and have decided to rise to the challenges.

If I am invited to do something I have never done before, I speak with Roland about it. If we both feel that I should accept the invitation, I do, even if I am nervous and even if it costs me a few nights without sleep. Wilhelm's invitation and encouragement was a steppingstone in my ministry.

MEN DISRESPECTING WOMEN

What I have shared so far may make it seem as if everything is easy in my part of the world, and as if women are included in the public ministry of the church on all levels of leadership. But, sadly, that is not the entire picture.

In my journey into ministry, I also experienced some things that made me very sad. One day, Roland and I were on our way to the south of

Germany, and he had to stop in order to be in a meeting of leaders in our country. I went with him to that meeting and sat in the back of the room, because he was only invited to speak for a few minutes to those leaders of large Christian organizations. After Roland had spoken, they took a break and wanted to continue a few minutes later. During that break, a well-respected leader in my country pointed to me and said to another leader, "Can we not show a film to this lady, so that she is not bored while we speak?" I was shocked. He did not talk to me, he talked about me, as if I were a little girl who was lost and needed help. My answer came quickly: "Oh, yes, please let us all watch the Heidi film together. I think we can all learn from it." He laughed, but I think he never realized how hurtful his words were and how much they showed about his attitude toward women. That would not have bothered me too much except for the fact that this man was in a leadership position over thousands of women in the churches he was representing, and that apparently he did not think very highly of women.

WORKING AS A TEAM

In our marriage, we have always worked as a team. Roland rejoices at the opportunities I have to serve the Lord. We are not competing. Because we do not have children due to my cancer treatment in 1989, we are both free to travel, to speak, and to be involved in different parts of the world. At the same time, we minister together in our church. People here know that we do not automatically agree on things. We are free to publicly voice conflicting opinions and to also criticize each other in love. At the same time, they know that we are the "greatest fans" of each other. I am proud of Roland and he is proud of me. I set him free to do what God has called him to do, and he does the same for me. I gladly submit to him as he gladly submits to me. But, to be honest, we do not often have to submit. We find a solution that is acceptable to both of us.

A few years back, I accepted the invitation to become the senior associate for women in evangelism with the Lausanne Movement. That was another big step in my life. How could God use a woman from Germany, a non-English speaking country, with no or very little funds, to fill such a position? Again, it was Roland and other male and female friends who encouraged me to take up this role. He was willing to let me go to different parts of the world, be separated for weeks, leaving him with the household chores for those times of the year.

ENCOURAGERS AND MENTORS

Another man who influenced my life is Leighton Ford, a well-known international Christian leader. Since 1993, Roland has been part of the Point Group, a group of leaders in evangelism from around the world whom Leighton brings together for a week of mentoring each year. Speaking about the Lausanne Congress in Manila in 1989 and about men and women working together back then, I have to add that Leighton was the leader of the Lausanne Movement at that time. He has always been an advocate for women in all roles in ministry. When I first met him, I was astonished at his way of treating men and women equally. Usually, men sit and talk to men and women sit together and talk. But with Leighton, it has always been different. It seems as if he does not even see the gender of the person he is talking to. He sees beyond. And he encourages the gifts he sees in people. After the Lausanne conference in Manila in 1989, he encouraged Robyn Claydon from Sidney, Australia, to travel the world and to help women to mentor women. And that is what Robyn did. She gave up her profession as a teacher and, for sixteen years, she travelled around the world as Lausanne's senior associate for women. In her travels, Robyn encouraged and mentored countless younger women. I was one of them.

Now, I follow in her footsteps. And I also work with Leighton Ford Ministries in mentoring younger leaders. I have a group of nine women from Germany, Austria, and Latvia whom I mentor right now. I am always blessed to meet with Leighton and the other mentors of mentors and to learn from him and them. Through them, I have understood more deeply that Christ sees beyond our roles; he sees our hearts.

My husband, Roland, is my best source of encouragement. He prays for me; when I travel, he calls me and is interested in what I do; he helps me with my English, as he lived and studied in the United States for a year when he was sixteen; he does the dishes and reads my articles or books before I hand them in. At the same time, he has his own ministry with youth, in evangelism and in mentoring younger men. In the last couple of years, Roland translated the New Testament into German, in translation similar to Eugene Peterson's *The Message*. He still travels a lot, and he is a wonderful leader in our church.

Every time I say goodbye and leave for another country, I am so thankful for my teammate, my husband. We are in this together. He is the man in my life who helps me to be the woman whom God intended me to be. And I pray and work hard to help other men and women in the Christian world to experience the same freedom and the same togetherness, because I believe that God made us this way. He created men and women to "do it together," to fulfill the creation mandate to take leadership in this world together (Gen 1). Truly, in Christ, "There is . . . neither male nor female, for you are all one in Christ Jesus" (Gal 3:28). I am so thankful for the men who are faithful to the Bible in this regard and encourage women to be all that God calls them to be in his kingdom.

7

Reflecting God's Image: A Father's Significance

Cynthia Davis Lathrop

JAMES BRYAN SMITH, IN his book *The Good and Beautiful God: Falling in Love with the God Jesus Knows*, states, "We are storied creatures, our stories help us navigate our world, to understand right and wrong and to provide meaning."[1] The stories I was told were pivotal in my life, helping me determine what I believed, how I behaved, and why I existed. When I was a child, my father told me stories about a character named "Bright Eyes," and these stories communicated my dad's values and beliefs. I listened to these stories and made them my own. Faithfulness, kindness, love, and courage were basic themes in my dad's tales. In this chapter, I want to share with you stories of my father and how he impacted my life.

My parents agreed before I was born that their words and actions needed to match if they were to be effective parents. While each of them had flaws, they did their best to live out what they taught. They wanted me and my siblings to become productive adults. From a human point of view, they were the ones responsible for molding and shaping me.

As I look back, I recognize the marvelous and lavish grace of God that flowed to me. During my formative years, I was learning about Jesus, but I had no understanding of grace. As I grew older, I came to realize that God was at work in me, revealing the heavenly Father to me through the loving relationship I had with my earthly father. This growing knowledge and love for my heavenly Parent has become the mainstay of my faith; it has given

---

1. Smith, *The Good and Beautiful God*, 25.

me confidence and trust in God's eternal character. I am thankful that Dad's life helped reveal and reflect some of the Lord's attributes to me.

My mother and father came from families where each of their parents worked outside the home. My grandmothers toughed it out, caring for their children, their spouses, the home, and their work responsibilities. My father held my grandmothers in high esteem. I was raised to recognize their strength of character, perseverance, and their love and sacrifice for their families.

When Dad and Mom married, they brought with them a multiplicity of ideas and experiences from each of their families. Together, they forged these into principles for living that they felt would be beneficial for their own family. By the time my parents, Ronald and Marjorie Davis, decided it was time to have children, they had already discussed the key ingredients a family needed: love, stability, and good models to follow. Their thoughts on these matters developed after each new plump, pink-cheeked addition came home to stay. In all, there would be four of us: me, my brother Jonathan, and my sisters, Penelope and Valerie.

I learned lessons of life over a period of twenty years, the years I lived in my parents' home. I learned important lessons by observing their marriage. During my teen years, I came to the conclusion that, if I married, I wanted to marry someone like my father. I admired the love and respect that I saw in his relationship with my mother. Though each of them had strong opinions, they shared similar goals and values. I saw that their mutual respect governed how they related to one another. To make family life fair, they decided to share household responsibilities. Dad washed dishes after supper, while Mom washed them in the morning. On weekends, Dad scrubbed the floors while Mom dusted and vacuumed. My father also did the laundry. My brother and I were involved in drying and folding clothes, which we often had to redo in order to meet Dad's specifications.

My mother enjoyed debating issues such as religion and politics. I remember numerous discussions at the dinner table. This helped me learn how to think independently. Dad encouraged this and I sensed his pride in Mom's political acumen. He was attentive and affirming as he listened to our conversations. When we had guests in our home or were guests elsewhere, Dad would raise issues that Mom was familiar with. Then, having opened the door for her, he would enjoy the dialogue. Mom's passion for politics was encouraged by my dad.

My parents' love for one another was evidenced by visible signs, such as a hug, a kiss, or a touch. These demonstrative signals made me feel secure in the knowledge of their love. Dad loved to tell us about his courtship of my mother. He described how he felt when he saw her, how he could recognize her by her walk, and when he knew that he loved her. We enjoyed these stories and pleaded with him to tell them to us again and again. I remember the flowers Dad bought for Mom on Saturday mornings. It became a game to guess the color of the carnations that he would bring home. Dad honored Mom by putting her first, and Mom did the same for Dad. Each of them told me how blessed I was to have the other as my parent.

When my grandfather died, we attended the burial at the cemetery. I stood behind my parents and watched them lean against one another, hands clasped behind their backs. Those intertwined fingers symbolized for me the oneness they shared, the special intimacy they had in all seasons of life.

I learned from my parents that a man and a woman are faithful to one another because of their commitment made before God. I came to view marriage as a true partnership, and the idea formed within me that only God could bring this partnership into being. I saw that mutual encouragement and support built confidence and trust in each of my parents. They were individuals who were interdependent partners.

Life with Dad also affected my spiritual life. My relationship with my father shaped my perception and experience of God. I believe that my dad, without ever knowing it, led me to seek intimacy with God. I loved spending time with Dad, and I wanted to spend time with God. Dad's behavior caused me to see God in the same way that I saw him: approachable, tenderhearted, and just.

We were members of the Episcopal Church, and Dad transported us there every week, even when he would have preferred to sleep late. It was in this church school that I learned the gospels and I came to think of Jesus as my friend. Here, I learned awe and reverence for God in the quiet of prayer amid the colorful stained-glass windows, and through my participation in choir. Dad also took us to Methodist, Congregational, Lutheran, and Catholic Church services. My parents wanted us to glimpse how other Christians worshipped.

At age fifteen I had a transforming experience, and I answered that soft voice that said, "Follow me." This opened up opportunities for me to discuss, and sometimes argue about, the Bible with my parents. Dad was an unusual man in that he always listened to me, no matter how different my opinions were from his. He heard me without criticizing or condemning me. I learned that I could always go to my father and tell him everything. This is how our relationship evolved as I went from childhood to adulthood, and this meant more to me than words can tell.

The best way I know to present you with a picture of my dad is to tell you the stories I remember of him. It was never just the words or jokes or circumstances that impacted me, but the transparent way he lived and loved.

GOOD MEDICINE

Dad had a cheerful heart (Ps 17:22). He dispensed cheerful medicine daily. We had a morning ritual—my dad, my brother, and me. Jonathan and I would sit in the hallway by the heater. Dad would be preparing for work, and we would hear him call, "Ow! Ow! It hurts! It hurts!" Jon and I knew what would happen next, so we tumbled over each other to get to Dad first. "It hurts to be so good looking!" Dad would exclaim with a wink.

Field trips were opportunities for Dad to engage with students and teachers. I would invite Dad to be a chaperone, and he would accept. Dad became an instant hit with my young schoolmates because he would do anything to get their attention and cause them to laugh. He would juggle fruit that we brought for snacks, tell outlandish stories with a serious face, or do a Highland Fling.[2] Dad was very good at putting everyone at ease and giving them something to talk about.

Humor and pranks went hand in hand with being a Davis. Family reunions are still spoken of with warmth and appreciation. My father and his brothers, George, Roderick, Robert, Hubert, and Jerrold, would clown around, set up games for us, sing and dance, and put on shows for all the cousins. My uncles were the ringleaders of laugher. As extended family, we strongly identified with our parents, aunts, and uncles. Family was a place to be loved and accepted.

I see now that Dad enjoyed life, and he enjoyed being with young people. In his enthusiasm for life, he was often criticized. But Dad was a man who was content to be himself. He taught me the importance of "being," and, as I grew in the things of God, I wanted to become the woman God had designed me to be.

2. A traditional Scottish dance.

COMPASSION

It was from my parents that I witnessed compassion in action. Dad was especially tenderhearted, and it showed as he comforted me when I grieved the loss of my grandmother. Even though I was just seven years old, he did not let me grieve alone. That was important to me: Dad did not ignore the pain and hurt I experienced, but he carried that pain also. My father was not one to speak at such times, and his appearance reflected his feeling of helplessness, but his presence with me soothed me and brought me peace. Does this not reflect the comfort and compassion of our God (2 Cor 1:4)? It was because of moments of connection like this that revelations of God's nature began to seep into my consciousness.

Dad also exhibited compassion outside our family. Often, we would visit the elderly and the sick in our neighborhood. Dad cheered those who seemed depressed and lifted the spirits of those who were homebound. He taught my cousin how to write again after my cousin survived a brain tumor. Because I loved my father, I wanted to be like him, and I began to seek out ways to help others. Even in this, the Holy Spirit was leading and developing our relationship with the Father and pointing us to the will of God for our lives.

RECONCILIATION

Scripture tells us that God disciplines those God loves (Heb 12:5–6). There were times my earthly father disciplined me, and now I am thankful for it, but when I was young, it was difficult to comprehend that love was the motivating factor.

Dad's deep love for our family encouraged him to participate in reconciliation when there was a family conflict. As I neared my teen years, I began to express myself in ways that were not always respectful to my mother. On one of those occasions, Dad was told about my actions, and he confronted me. Dad did not raise his voice, but he called me into a separate room. We stood staring at one another. I had no desire to link eyes with him. I knew his eyes would broadcast the disappointment and sorrow he felt at that moment. I felt guilty for my words and attitude.

Dad remained silent, studying my face. He peered intently into my eyes and quietly asked, "Why, Cynthia? Why speak this way? She is your mother." I had no answer. Dad's kindness broke the rebellion in me. I cried, and Dad put his arms around me. "You need to apologize and ask your mother to forgive you," he told me. Then he patted me on the shoulder and expected me to obey—and I did.

Dad's kindness to me was a reflection of the kindness of God (Rom 2:4). His discipline was redemptive, allowing me to be molded more closely into the image of our Lord Jesus Christ. Once again, Dad's example and the grace of God were working together through the Holy Spirit. God used the simple, common, day-to-day occurrences with my father to prepare and equip me for a fuller revelation of the God who knew me as a person and who had plans for my life.

PERSEVERANCE

My father set an example of hard work and perseverance. In his job as an accountant, he commuted daily more than thirty miles each way from Danbury, Connecticut, to Stratford, Connecticut, working long hours and arriving home late most evenings. Sickness was not an excuse for him to miss work, and these values somehow transferred to me in my educational and extracurricular activities.

Dad also persevered in his relationship with me. As his child, when he held my hand, I knew I was loved and protected. When dad sat at the table helping me with my math, I knew he was sacrificing his time to invest in my future. Taking walks on Interstate 84 when it was nothing more than hard-packed earth gave us time to share and tell stories. Dad had an enthusiastic hope, which he passed on to me.

As I grew up in my father's house, he would praise my strengths and support my attempts to become my own person. When times came when I wanted to quit, Dad would talk me into sticking it out. "You can do it," he would tell me. "If not you, then who?" he would demand. There was no way that I wanted to disappoint Dad, so I would try again. In truth, my father taught me by his life that love " . . . always protects, always trusts, always hopes, always perseveres" (1 Cor 13:7 TNIV).

My dad's humanity endeared him to me. He did not always have answers for all my questions, but he was honest about it. He did not have perfect patience, joy, or peace. Dad was simply Dad, and his life pointed me to the one who is always perfect and good.

During my high school years, Dad was my advocate, standing by my decisions to study science, history, and music. He challenged me to become a better swimmer by giving me opportunities to stretch my endurance, and he would swim beside me at times when I was completely exhausted. When I showed an interest in something new, Dad cheered me on; if I was afraid, Dad encouraged me to do it anyway. There have been many times I've asked myself how my dad did these things. I tell you frankly that I do not know. But this I do know: My father loved me, and I trusted him. He loved each of his children, and he did his best to give us the support and opportunities to blossom into the persons we were called to be.

LESSONS LEARNED FROM MY PARENTS' MARRIAGE

From my parents' marriage, I learned that love and respect were mutual, sharing responsibility was fair, love was visible and verbal, and marriage was a partnership birthed by God. This has consequences for my relationship with God today, as an individual and as a member of the global body of Christ. I am to love God with all that is within me, and the global church is to love God wholly, too. Awe and reverence are needed to approach a loving, holy God. As coheirs with Christ, women and men serve together, sharing the responsibility of advancing the reign of God, and we do this by using the gifts God has given us. Our love for God is visible in how we treat each other as brothers and sisters, and it is verbal as we come together to lift our voices in giving God all the praise and glory God deserves. Some day, Jesus will return for his bride, the church, and this mysterious relationship will be consummated as we surrender to the lover of our souls.

LESSONS LEARNED FROM MY RELATIONSHIP WITH DAD

Family was important to my father. He did all he could to encourage our love and loyalty to one another. The same is true in God's kingdom. God desires our love and loyalty also, and then commands us to love and serve one another.

What I have learned from my dad and try to practice in my life is perseverance. The journey is a process, and I am committed to loving God and putting God's word and will first in my life. This includes my marriage and partnership with my husband, John, along with our children and grandchildren.

This process includes loving, laughing, and crying with others, encouraging and supporting people as they step out to use their gifts and abilities for God's service. It means preferring others before me. It is yielding to Christ and reflecting him so that his light shines forth from me.

For this to happen, I have learned I must surrender all that I am to God. Pride would stay my hand. But what is reputation or ambition, what is fame or fortune, celebrity or admiration or prominence, if Christ does not receive all the glory?

What I learned from my dad is that I must decrease and Christ must increase. This holds true for everyone, whether they are female or male, slave or free, Jew or Gentile. Each of us must be what God calls us to be, and we must be humble while we do the work of God.

8

On Rising Up Above the Refugee Tent

KeumJu Jewel Hyun

I JUST RETURNED FROM my ninth trip to Kenya after holding two conferences to train pastors and church leaders who had not received formal
theological and biblical training due to financial difficulties. I am neither
a typical Korean American woman nor a typical housewife. I founded
Matthew 28 Ministries, Inc., a nonprofit organization that focuses on
training women in Kenya to be effective in their ministries in the church
and in the community. I started seminary studies after taking early retirement from a nearly thirty-year career. The ensuing seven years of studies
culminated in my earning two degrees, a master's degree and a doctoral
degree.

This took place at the age when most men and women would enjoy their retirement after a long career. It was all possible because, by the
grace of God, I have been surrounded with many uniquely supportive
and understanding men. Among them, my father, my husband, and the
senior pastor of my former home church stand out.

My father was unique and countercultural. My maternal grandfather
had many concubines and neglected his wife and children because my
grandmother did not bear him any sons. When my brother was born, my
grandfather named his favorite fruit tree in his orchard after my brother,
but none for me, because I was a girl. However, my father raised me with
no gender distinctions or limitations in terms of ability. He taught me
never to think I was inferior to boys just because I was a girl. Perhaps that

is why I have never been intimidated by any man. My husband, whose mother was a successful, professional career woman, considers me as an equal partner in our marriage, supporting me to be successful in all I do and having discovered God-given gifts in me. He is the chief "promoter" of my ministry work. My pastor was unique because he saw the potential in me as God saw me and equipped me to serve the church. Having been privileged with such supportive men throughout my life, I am compelled to share the stories of how these three men influenced me and shaped my life.

MY FATHER, SANG HOON LEE

I was born in a small fishery town in the northern part of the Korean peninsula when the country was under the oppression of Japanese colonialism. After thirty-six years of occupation, Korea was liberated from Japan only to be divided into two Koreas: North Korea under the supervision of the Soviet Union and South Korea under the supervision of the United States of America. Thus, North Korea became a communist country and South Korea enjoyed the freedom of a democracy. At that time, my father was a banker, vice president of a communist, government-run bank. He was not an ordinary father; he was different from my friends' fathers. His ideology led him to choose to be a member of the Democratic Party when everyone else belonged to the Communist Party. My mother was a homemaker and a Christian in a communist regime. For this reason, the communist officials hated us and kept us under constant surveillance.

We lived in the vice presidential mansion, a huge, Japanese-style house. Although the house had many rooms, our family of five lived in one room as a normal family would do. Then, one day, my father showed me one of the rooms in the house and told me that someday that room would be mine. In those days, there was no concept of children having their own rooms. Nevertheless, my father set aside one room for me! He was different. I remember thinking about the room for many days and waiting for the day to come when I would have my own room. One of the largest rooms in the house was my father's study, lined with many books, a radio—his favorite item—and a large table, which he used as a desk whenever he taught me English or algebra.

The government assigned a Russian army officer as father's attaché, whom we called Uncle Masha. I do not know why he was assigned to my father, whether because he was a bank officer or because our family was on their "watch list." Regardless, Uncle Masha seemed to be always around our house even though he did not live with us. He was very friendly, and my brother and I loved playing with him whenever he did not have to talk with my father. Uncle Masha taught me how to count in Russian, and my father started teaching some Russian vocabulary words. Then one day, suddenly, my father started teaching me English instead of Russian! Later, I learned from my mother that Uncle Masha had told my father that there was no hope and future with the Soviet Union; thus, my father ought to teach me English instead of Russian. How prophetic Uncle Masha was! My father's teaching me English was interrupted when the Korean War broke out, but it foreshadowed the teaching that he would resume during my life as a refugee. Who would have thought that learning English in North Korea would serve me well in South Korea later!

My father's devotion to me was beyond description. I remember the days when my brother and I sat down with him right outside of his study and shaped plates, tea cups and saucers, and pots and pans out of clay for my playhouse. We then baked them in a charcoal hibachi. Where did he find the time? I just enjoyed spending time with him. At the same time, I revered him. I would not do anything that would not please him or might get him upset or disappoint him. I trusted that he would do anything for us, and I believed everything he told us. This childhood experience helped me to understand better what it means "to fear the Lord" and trust my heavenly Father.

My father started teaching me algebra when I was in the second grade. Every day after dinner, I would go to his study and start solving algebra problems. There were many nights when I was in tears simply because I could not understand some of the problems and was intimidated by the complexity of the algebra equations. Nevertheless, I enjoyed studying algebra. Just as I was about to brag about my advanced knowledge of algebra, I contracted a contagious disease in an epidemic, and I was placed in quarantine. It was the beginning of my third grade year. One day, on his way home from a business trip, my father came to visit me at the place where I was quarantined. I was really excited to see him. I expected that he would bring me a nice gift since I was sick and away from home. However, to my amazement, he brought none other than an algebra textbook! I still remember how disappointed I was!

Even though he did not have a college education, my father had deep knowledge about many subjects—classical music, photography, museums, and astronomy, to name a few. He had his own darkroom for his photography, and I was fascinated to see pictures coming out of a dish with nothing but some chemical solution in it. He told me the most important aspect of photography is "composition"; however, for some reason to this date, I have not developed an interest in photography. However, I still love classical music and visiting museums.

Some nights, my brother and I went outside with my father to look at the stars. The skies were filled with bright stars and were breathtakingly crisp; my mind raced with the speed of the twinkling of the stars to the land where only a child's imagination can take it. There, my father would teach the various positions and names of stars, the theory of the galaxy, and the solar system. He explained many of the stars, pointing out the Big Dipper, Little Dipper, and the North Star at the end of the Little Dipper "handle." I was so fascinated that I wanted to be an astronomer when I grew up. Other nights, he would read us books of detective stories about Sir Yoo BooLan, a Korean equivalent of Sherlock Holmes. Although I do not remember any specifics of the stories, I was intrigued by the thrill and excitement; it was a great treat for me. Perhaps that is why I love to watch the reruns of *Murder She Wrote*.

Alas! My happy childhood was abruptly disrupted by the Korean War.[1] Bombs were dropped from fighter planes like raindrops falling from the sky. Every time we heard the sound of airplanes, we ran for our lives and hid in foxholes, often stumbling over corpses as we ran. To this date, the airplane sound reminds me of those days and gives me goose bumps. After living six months of such a horrendous life, we enjoyed the peace and freedom that was brought to us by General Douglas Macarthur's successful landing at Incheon harbor. Sadly, the freedom did not last. Soon, we were on board a train being evacuated by United Nations soldiers as they withdrew from the fierce battle. The train took us to a harbor where United States navy carriers waited for us to embark to be evacuated to South Korea.

---

1. Although American government considers it as an internal "conflict" like a civil war, we always considered it as a war between communism and democracy. We were taught that the Soviet Union invaded South Korea to unify the entire Korean peninsula as a communist country.

On board the ship, we lived on one small ball of rice per day; after thirteen days of hardship, we arrived at an island in South Korea. We were then transported to a refugee camp where tents were pitched in a schoolyard. In the tent, each family had a designated spot. That small area served as our new "home" for the next several months. Each day, my brother and I went out with a gallon-size can to the feeding station and lined up for food provided by the ministry of Rev. Bob Pierce, who later founded World Vision. The food was rationed to children only; our parents, along with my two baby sisters, shared the food that my brother and I brought. Because the food was not enough for all of us, my father regulated the portion by telling us to stop eating according to the age, the youngest one eating the least. Since many families shared the tent, life in the tent was utterly chaotic: babies were crying, kids were screaming all the time, things were stolen, and people were fighting and arguing. There was no regard for other people. It was just miserable to live there. Nevertheless, the faithful God governed my life with his providence and guided me with goodness such that this refugee girl eventually earned a doctoral degree from a seminary many years later!

Although we did not own anything, we had one item precious to us: a photograph of Uncle Masah, which was mixed in the family photographs we brought when we fled. We guarded the picture of him very carefully because, not only was he dear to us, but also we feared that if someone found out that he was a Russian army officer, we would be arrested and be put into jail. Thankfully, it never happened!

We eventually moved out of the refugee tent and moved in with a native South Korean family. This generous family took us in and let us use one of the rooms in the house; in return, my mother helped them with chores on their farm, planting seeds, pulling weeds from rice fields, and harvesting and winnowing grains. My father had a job as a Korean-English translator at the United States prisoner of war camp, where he worked during the week and came home on weekends. Since we were still refugees, my parents could not afford to send me to school. Consequently, my father resumed teaching me English, which he had started when Uncle Masah prophetically told him to years earlier in North Korea. He would teach on weekends and give me homework to do during the weekdays.

My parents finally settled in a tungsten mine village. There was a large army charcoal storage station guarded around the clock by United Nations military police. Sometimes, I would walk up to the entrance gate and practice my English, saying whatever I had memorized and could remember. I became acquainted with some of the soldiers there. One day, when I walked up there, a solider gave me something wrapped in yellow paper and told me I could eat it. I unwrapped and ate it. It was heavenly! It was the first time I had ever tasted something so good: chocolate! Later, I found out that it was a Butterfinger chocolate bar. Even today, Butterfinger is my favorite chocolate; every day, I eat a bite-size piece as an after-dinner dessert. I also take a bag of Butterfingers every time I go to Kenya, thinking of those days.

My father had a job at the chemical research laboratory at the tungsten mine, and my parents finally were able to send me to school. It was the first time I would ever set foot in a classroom in South Korea. The only education I had received up to that point was completing the second grade of elementary school in North Korea; most of my third-grade year was spent in quarantine, and my fourth-grade year was interrupted by the war. One day, my mother took me to the middle school, where I passed their test by translating simple English sentences into Korean. My father's teaching me English had paid off. After a long disruption, my schooling in South Korea began in the last month of the seventh grade. Having missed more than three years of education—the fourth through sixth grades and almost all of the seventh grade—I was hungry to study. There, I excelled, not only in English and mathematics, but also in other subjects. I enjoyed studying; I still love to study and learn new subjects.

As I resumed my education at the middle school, I also started going to church and joined the youth group. There were many girls and boys in the youth group who had fled North Korea as I did. Being from the northwestern part of North Korea, where Christianity entered Korea, these boys and girls knew a lot about the Bible and had spiritual disciplines; they very much influenced my spiritual life. While my mother and I were active at church, my father did not go to church; he was not even a Christian.[2] However, it did not bother me at that time, because he was very knowledgeable of the Bible. In fact, he is the one who led me to believe that Jesus was a historical figure and that resurrection of Jesus was a real event that had taken place.

---

2. Almost three decades later, he accepted Jesus Christ as his personal Savior and was baptized at the church, of which my husband and I were the founding members. A few years later he passed on to be with the Lord.

Upon graduation from the middle school, I decided to go to Seoul for my high school education and submitted application to Ewha Girls' High School, a private school founded by an American missionary. The competition was fierce, and entrance examinations were very hard. I did not do well overall; however, I was accepted because my English and mathematics scores were very good. Apparently, those two subjects weighed fifty percent of the total score of the entrance examinations. My father's efforts in teaching me English and algebra at an early age had paid off again enormously. In my sophomore year, Rev. Bob Pierce came to Korea and held a revival meeting in Seoul. Having been fed by his ministry staff many years ago at the refugee camp, I went to hear him preach at the revival meeting. That night, when he made an altar call, I accepted Jesus Christ as my personal Savior and Lord. Later, it occurred to me that Rev. Bob Pierce nourished me not only with physical food, but also with spiritual food.

I loved my father very much; I wanted to do anything that would please him. I even thought that he would never die. He made me feel that I was the most important person to him in the whole world. He had never said he did not have time for me; he just enjoyed devoting his time and energy to me. Having had such a devoted father, I sense a reality when I read the Scripture on my heavenly Father's love for me and his protection of me as the apple of his eye. My father was truly my hero.

MEET MY HUSBAND, CHUL WOO "GENE" HYUN

In my junior year in college, I met my future husband, Gene. We were married when we each earned a master's degree in nuclear physics from Yonsei University. Upon graduation, we came to America to pursue doctorate degrees in nuclear physics. However, the circumstances did not allow us to continue our studies; we diverted our concentration to the computer field and were trained accordingly. We started working in information technology—Gene as a software engineer and I as a programmer in business applications. My first assignment was to support a banking system that was written in Assembler language, one of the most difficult computer languages to learn. I knew nothing about the language; I brought home all the manuals I could find and asked Gene to help. He started studying the new computer language on top of his own workload. Within a week, he mastered the language and taught me how to do the programming in Assembler language. When my boss saw my progress, he thought I could walk on water!

Throughout my career, Gene has been my tutor, advocate, and my advisor. He was supportive of my career; he wanted me to succeed in all I did. He was available to help me in juggling my career and raising the children. He took care of all that needed to be done at home when I had to work for extended hours, many times around the clock. At one time, having worked many years in corporate America, I was burned out and tired of what I was doing. I wanted to do something different; I wanted to quit the job and open a dry cleaning shop! I wonder what would have happened to me had I indeed pursued the idea. One thing for sure, we would have been under a great financial burden as our children were in college and in private high school then. Even so, Gene did not dismiss my plans as preposterous; rather, he took me seriously and gladly collaborated with me weighing the implications. He was supportive of me because he respected my reasoning and trusted me that I would not make a foolish, self-centered decision. He stood by me until I came to my senses and realized that making such a radical change might not be a good thing for fulfilling the will of God for me.

When we were spiritually dry, we learned of a pastor who was thinking of planting a church. Gene and I joined the pastor along with some friends of ours and started the first Korean Presbyterian church in Boston. We became active in Bible study, teaching the Sunday school, and serving the newly immigrated Koreans. One day, both Gene and I were in a committee meeting of this newly founded church, where I did not hesitate to express my opinion on a certain subject. After the meeting, one of the men came up to Gene and told him something like, "Tell your wife to be silent in the meeting." In Korean custom in such a case, the husband would get very upset with the wife because she had embarrassed him; he would rebuke her and tell her not to say anything in future meetings. However, Gene would not have it. Gene told me later that he had said to the man, "*You* tell her that." For him, I was not just his wife, but also an individual human being who deserved to be respected in her own right. Well, the man has never come up to tell me personally!

As I was growing in my spiritual journey, I became interested in serving and teaching the Bible outside of church, particularly to incarcerated girls. When an opportunity came to teach the Bible at a juvenile prison, Gene gladly joined me to co-teach at one of the most heavily guarded juvenile prisons in the Commonwealth of Massachusetts. We served the teenage girls teaching the Bible for the next seven years. As I was teaching, I felt the inadequacy of my knowledge of the Bible and wished to take some seminary courses to enrich my ministry to those girls. However, the circumstances did not allow me to consider it seriously. Then, one day, when we were discussing things about our work, unexpectedly, Gene suggested considering pursuing seminary studies to develop and utilize further God-given gifts. He said that he had noticed the gift of teaching in me while we were teaching the Bible at the prison. If I were to pursue these studies, I would have to close the consulting firm that I had founded a few years earlier; we would have reduced income. To him, my studying at a seminary was more valuable than earning extra income. By then, our children were out of school and had their own careers, and we would not have any financial burden like a few years earlier. I thought it was confirmation from God that I should study because I had been thinking about it for a long time. I immediately started the process and enrolled in the master's program at Gordon-Conwell Theological Seminary. Here, a husband was willing to sacrifice financially and support his wife to be equipped for better service for Christ in ministry. I think that discovering God's gifts in a wife is an expression of a husband's love for her as Christ's love for the church (Eph 5:25). I was grateful to God for him.

While I was a seminarian, I was talking with a Korean pastor who was well known in the Boston area and shared with him my excitement about seminary studies. Contrary to Gene, as a typical Korean man would say, he told me that he did not understand why a woman wanted to study at a seminary. His comment was not unusual in a Korean context. In that culture, supporting a wife's seminary studies is an extraordinary thing for a Korean man to do. Gene was and is countercultural, just like Jesus was when he was on earth.

During my seminary years, everything I learned in the classroom was new and exciting. I could not wait to share what I learned with Gene: new Greek vocabulary words, new theological terminology, principles of interpretation of the Bible, and other topics. He was excited because I enjoyed my studies so much; once, he said that we were two seminarians even though we were paying the tuition for one student. Gene never said he was not interested in what I had to say about what I had learned. In fact, I do not remember that he ever said either that he did not have the time or was not interested in listening to what I had to say. He is a great listener. With Gene's great support, I studied at the seminary for seven years, earning a master's degree in New Testament and a doctor of ministry degree in effective ministries to women.

MY PASTOR, REV. EVERETT F. REED

The seed of my interest in seminary studies was planted when we attended an Anglo church. As we were actively serving the newly planted Korean church, Gene was diagnosed with hepatitis B and required complete rest; at the most he could sit up a little longer than one hour. In order to accommodate his needs, we decided to attend a church nearby. We started attending the First Baptist Church of Wilmington, where our children had been attending the Sunday school with our next-door neighbor. Switching from the Korean ethnic church to an Anglo church was not an easy transition; whether singing hymns or listening to sermons, each time we had to make a mental translation from Korean to English. Nevertheless, the church ministered to us dearly, and we were blessed immensely. It was in this church that my doctrinal understanding was solidified and my spiritual journey was further enriched. The senior pastor, Rev. Everett F. Reed, was young and had not been there very long when we joined the church. I had thought that Calvin's TULIP[3] was the only theological doctrine that existed and had believed that everyone accepted it, until I noticed that the Baptists did not talk much about it. Pastor Reed was patient with me whenever I challenged him about the Baptist doctrine with my limited understanding of Calvinism. He not only was patient with me, but also nurtured the God-given gifts in me.

Pastor Reed saw the potential in me as God saw and equipped me to serve the church through teaching the Bible. He courageously assigned me to teach a coed adult class when not only our family was relatively new to the church but also I had no experience of teaching the Bible to adults. He gave me full support and allowed me to use his library for any references that I would need to prepare for the class. One Sunday, a woman visitor sat in my class and did not like what she saw—a woman teaching the Bible to a class with men in it. After the class, she called me aside and rebuked me, quoting 1 Timothy 2:12: "I do not permit a woman to teach or to have authority over a man. . . ." She said that I had violated that verse.

3. TULIP is an acronym for Total depravity, Unconditional election, Limited atonement, Irresistible grace, and Perseverance of the saints.

In fact, I was not even aware of the controversy of 1 Timothy 2:12 until then. After the worship service, I informed my pastor of the incident. Pastor Reed took the time, went through the entire Bible, and pointed out the passages that support women's teaching. On one occasion, Pastor Reed asked me to substitute-teach his Wednesday evening Bible study when he had a conflict in his schedule. The subject of the night happened to be the Trinity! He did not have any doubt about whether I would be able to teach such a difficult subject. He trusted that I would study hard and be prepared as well as I could be with my ability. He gave me an opportunity to demonstrate my potential.

One year, we were doing a topical Bible study when Pastor Reed told us that Gordon-Conwell Theological Seminary offered a course on that particular subject, and that he could take us to audit some classes if anyone was interested. I had no idea until then that anyone, even if they had been out of school a long time, could take a seminary course, audit or not. It was quite a revelation, and it planted a seed in my heart for seminary studies. Eventually, Gene and I enrolled in and completed the lay leadership certificate program at Ockenga Institute of the seminary. Then, when the right time came, I enrolled in a degree program.

When we decided to go back to the Korean church, Pastor Reed sent us as "missionaries" trained in Anglo culture to serve Christ by ministering to people of Korean culture. Gene and I started teaching the Bible to the college students back in the Korean church. These students, children of Korean immigrants, were bicultural—living in the Western culture with Korean heritage. Some of them were experiencing difficulties in adjusting to a new culture at the universities they attended. Having been trained in an Anglo church and exposed to Western culture at work, we were able to relate and minister to them effectively. We benefited a great deal from our ten-year exposure to Christianity in the Western culture through the First Baptist Church of Wilmington. The experience gained at the church prepared me to be effective in ministering cross-culturally today. Pastor Reed truly nurtured me to grow and influenced me immensely in becoming who I am today. I thank God for him.

As I become involved in ministries, Gene continues to be my advocate, advisor, and benefactor. He accompanies me on trips, whether fundraising, donor development, or speaking. He has been to Kenya twice; I know I can count on him whenever I need his help, and he is ready to extend his helping hand. He is truly a partner in ministry, and I am thankful to God that he is my husband.

A REFLECTION

As I look back at my life, my father, my husband, and the pastor of my former home church each played a significant role for me to become who I am. Through my father's love and devotion to me, I have better knowledge of God's character—his everlasting love and trustworthiness. Because I had such deep fatherly love, I can relate to a degree to God as a loving, caring, and nurturing Father. Whenever I read the "fear of God" in the Bible, I can understand the meaning of it because I revered my father while maintaining close relationship with him as a daughter. I thought my father was a walking "encyclopedia" to whom I could come with questions on any subject, but my heavenly Father is omniscient. I can come to my heavenly Father any time for guidance or joy to share as I used to do with my earthly father. My earthly father trained me, without knowing it, for me to enjoy the love and grace of my heavenly Father.

Through my husband, I learned that equal partnership in marriage develops into equal partnership in ministry. I also learned the importance and significance of men and women being able to work and grow together in ministry, recognizing and respecting each other's gifts. I often wonder how Gene was able to support me in an extraordinary way. I do not have one particular answer, but I can say easily that, aside from his love for his wife, Gene knows and firmly believes that God created man and woman equally, and that "There is neither Jew nor Greek, slave nor free, male nor female" and all are "one in Christ Jesus" (Gal 3:28 NIV). To him, I am a woman, a person, who happens to be his wife. Thus, there is no stereotypical male domineering trait in him. How thankful I am to be married to him!

Pastor Reed taught me what a ministry leader can do to nurture a saint to grow and be equipped for the work of ministry. He patiently guided me when I did not adjust well in the transition from a Presbyterian upbringing to the Baptist community. In the meantime, he discovered God-given gifts in me and helped me to develop, and he gave me opportunities to utilize these gifts. He did not keep me from serving the church in certain areas just because I am a woman. To him, I was a member in his flock who happens to be a woman whom he was equally responsible for equipping for ministry.

Indeed, I was blessed with exceptionally supportive godly men. I believe God surrounded me with these men with a purpose: for me to serve the women in Africa and other parts of the world who do not receive such support from men. I am grateful to my Lord for such privilege. To God be the glory.

9

How a Man Can Help His Wife
Become the Person God Intended

Aída Besançon Spencer

YEARS AGO, WHEN OUR son was young, I played a final basketball competition with our son's friend at our home. Whenever I came up to throw the ball into the hoop, our son's friend yelled out discouraging comments like, "You can't do it," "You're going to miss," and, although my aim was normally good, it quickly deteriorated to very bad. Then, my husband, Bill, came outside and started yelling out encouraging comments like "You can do it," "This is easy for you," "You're really good at this," and immediately my aim improved. How could a little kid have discouraged me so? And how could simple but honest words of confidence have encouraged me so soon? Nevertheless, even as an adult, I have felt immediately the effect of my environment. That's what my husband and, to some extent, even my father did for me—they set up environments of possibility that helped me become who God intended me to be. God's name is "I will be who I will be" (Exod 3:14, my translation), and God working through these men helped me be what I could be.

When I worked in Trenton State maximum security prison, I had the same philosophy for the inmates: Treat them as you want them to become, and they will become it. In the same way, the Apostle Paul exhorted husbands to love their wives as Christ loved the church, helping their wives to become the cleansed and holy royal priests who proclaim the mighty acts of God (Eph 5:25–27, 1 Pet 2:9). Bill treated me like a princess made in God's image, and thus all my gifts slowly actualized.

From a princess, I became royalty in God's kingdom. Our life together can be organized under six time periods: (1) getting to know each other and adapting ideas, (2) working together to be trained, (3) encouraging each other in our callings, (4) resolving familial issues, (5) dealing with challenges in work, and (6) planning for mature development.

GETTING TO KNOW EACH OTHER AND ADAPTING IDEAS

Like most parents, my parents had their strengths and weaknesses in dealing with me, their child. Their strength was that they assumed I could be whatever I wanted. Their desires for me were their desires for themselves. My father, a comptroller for the Curacao Trading Company, was for a while a consul for the Netherlands while in the Dominican Republic. Thus, he wanted me to become an ambassador (a greater position even than consul). My mother, who raised French poodles and read the *Merck Manual*[1] for bedtime reading, wanted me to become a veterinarian. Although gifted in political science, I shrank away from sticky political scenes. And, although I trimmed the poodles, I fainted at the sight of gushing blood. Even though those particular vocations were not fully suited to my strengths, I did learn that I could pursue any vocation I desired.

But, at times I felt like a slave in my own home. Even though she reared me in the Dominican Republic with household servants (a nanny when I was young, a cook, a house cleaner, a clothes washer, and a gardener), my mother made me work constantly too around the house. At first I thought it unnecessary and unjust, but now I can see that my mother trained me to be a hard worker. When we were in the Dominican Republic, the system worked relatively well because many people visited us. As they chatted on the porch, I then scurried away and played—roller skating around the house and climbing trees. But, when we moved to New Jersey, where my mother had no household servants and few people visited, where life was closed in, I became the only household helper my mother had. During high school years, we lived far away from downtown and my school. Without my mother bringing me, I had no place to which I could go. Day after day, I would do each household job, and, before I was done, my mother had another job, and then another job, hour after hour, day after day, week after week, month after month. I felt so confined. My mother, who blossomed

---

1. A medical reference book for diagnosis and therapy.

in the Dominican Republic with a team of workers under her and with continual well-wishers who dropped by, was now a Puerto Rican foreigner constricted to her own house. Thus, in despair, I slowly turned inward. Like the Israelites, I felt I had too oppressive a taskmaster.

Once, when in college, I returned home for the weekend. When Bill came to pick me up, he could see that I had retreated from being the woman who "could be" to the woman of "never becoming." I had quickly shrunk back into a seed. Bill helped that seed blossom. We met in college at an InterVarsity Christian Fellowship retreat. We rode together in the car that brought a group of Douglass and Rutgers students to Hudson House in New York, I in the front seat, Bill with two others in the back. Although he did not notice me in the car the first night (he says because that night included his first visit to a woman's dormitory and he was over-whelmed!), the next day, we met during the Saturday afternoon hike up the mountain. The Holy Spirit directed us to each other, and we chat-ted up and down the small mountain about the questions, "What is real? What is a life of integrity?" Bill respected my thoughts, and I felt delighted to dialogue with a reflective man. On the basis of dialogue and mutual respect, we built our relationship. Instead of feeling limited, I now felt en-couraged to think and to envision. Bill was certainly different from some other fellows that I dated. I remember another Rutgers man saying that I thought too much (which, translated, meant: Let's be physical only!). But, Bill never said that.

As a sociology major, I was taught to evaluate people in difficulties from the larger societal perspective. Thus, I did not blame every person receiving welfare benefits as too lazy to work, as was common in the 1950s and 1960s. After a while, to avoid conflict-laden meals with my parents, I did not participate in home discussions on the topic. My first (and probably only) convert was my husband. I remember the moment. I was trying to explain how societal discrimination can oppress and limit people. As we turned the corner, I glanced at Bill, who was driving, and, after a pause, he turned to me and said, "I see what you mean. I agree." I was dumbfounded!

We met in 1966, but we were married in 1972. During those years, we talked about many issues, including the roles of men and women. We learned about our weaknesses and strengths. Slowly, we began to meld together our ideas and our practices. Bill helped me make a solid commit-ment to the Lord when he asked me, "Do you know that you are saved?"

and he added, "The Lord of the universe is waiting for your answer!" I certainly did not want to keep the Lord of the universe waiting! Anyway, who was more trustworthy than Jesus? The next morning, I knelt by my bed and asked Jesus to forgive me and become my trustworthy Lord.

WORKING TOGETHER TO BE TRAINED

I was brought up in a Protestant church in a Roman Catholic country. (The Dominican Republic, by the way, is the only country in the world with the Bible on its flag.) I had never met a fundamentalist until I was in high school. One afternoon after school, I had a discussion with another Christian about whether Christians had to listen to Christian radio. She asked me if I did (as if that would help me). Despite my limited knowledge, I told her that listening to Christian radio was not indispensable to being a Christian. She ended up agreeing. Already then, I was making a distinction between the Christian culture and Christ. Nevertheless, despite my hesitations, over the years, in high school and college, I slowly formed the impression that women should be more passive and men more active (even though I attended an all women's college!). Men were somehow supposed to be in the coed leadership positions. Men were supposed to teach the Bible. Men were supposed to lead in the home. This influence came not only from the religious community, but also from the secular community. For example, when at home, I used to pick up my father at the train station whenever I borrowed the family car. I noticed that almost every woman who drove to pick up her husband, after turning off the car, dragged herself over to the passenger side to allow her husband to drive them home. Night after night I observed this curious practice. Finally, I began to wonder if my father might be insulted because I did not let him drive. So, one night, I dragged myself over to the passenger seat before he arrived. When he came, he looked into the passenger's window, puzzled, and asked why I was sitting there. After I explained, he said, "Ah, no, you drive!" and he settled himself into the passenger seat while I drove us home. Through the years, that was a defining moment in my life. Imitating the larger culture was not always worth it because my father was proud to have a daughter who drove him around. He had confidence in my abilities.

When I finished college, I worked for a year as a community organizer for Latin Americans. Bill, on the other hand, went right from college to seminary. I lived in Scotch Plains, New Jersey, with my parents, while he commuted to Philadelphia, attending Conwell School of Theology.[2] Each weekend, he would tell me about his courses, and I would be so interested in the subject matter. Although I enjoyed my work, helping people find the resources for their needs, I thought that, in the long run, I was simply helping the poor become middle class. Helping people with their economic needs was worthwhile, but it was not enough. So, Bill began to encourage me to attend seminary with him in Philadelphia. I asked him if women attended, and his answer was, "Yes! By all means!" (As it turned out, one nurse was attending one of his classes.) I honestly did not know, but I had a vague feeling that it was not common. Since I had been severely underpaid, I said I needed a scholarship to attend. Bill said he would help, and he did. We set a Saturday to go to Philadelphia, about a three-hour ride. We arrived in the evening, and Bill managed to find the street where the school president lived. It was a street looming up and down with identical row-townhouses. Bill finally narrowed his choice to two houses that might be the home of the president, Stuart Barton Babbage. I indicated the house on the right, as the Holy Spirit seemed to direct me. We knocked. A baffled and surprised Dr. Babbage came to the door. He and his wife had been traveling all summer and just happened to be home for an hour between travels. He was so surprised that we caught him at home that he gave me that scholarship that very night. If today Bill were to tell me, "Let's go to Philadelphia, not letting anyone know we are coming and not exactly knowing where we are going, and let's speak to a seminary president about getting money for some unknown student, since I've been studying part of one semester," I would be dismayed at such apparent disorganization and incompetence and never go. But "I will be who I will be" is a sovereign God who is always acting and always near. God guided us as Bill encouraged me, not only in words, but also in action.

While in college and seminary, I attended a Presbyterian church that allowed women to minister. But, one day, the head pastor said to me as he, I, Bill, and a male friend entered the church building, "It's good that you are going to seminary, but it's even more important for the men to go." Then, he left my side and moved up to walk with Bill and our friend, leaving me straggling behind. The two young men were paid as seminary interns and were made responsible for church programs. I was asked to teach a youth Bible class (for free). I do not think Bill by himself (then) would have

2. Conwell School of Theology merged with Gordon Divinity School in 1969 to become Gordon-Conwell Theological Seminary.

noticed the inconsistency. He was simply zealous to serve God. With others, he started a coffeehouse outreach that met every night and, of course, he encouraged me to join him in this ministry. However, when we attended Christian social events, I would feel abandoned as he greeted everyone and seemed to forget I was there. His goal was to serve God—that came first. But, I found some quiet time with him and explained that I felt we needed some time for the two of us alone. I also shared how I felt ignored on social occasions. As a result, we carved out some time for our own relationship and, when we did socialize, Bill made a point of including me in the conversations. Even today, after all these years of marriage, we still allot normally two nights each week for us to relax together, and Bill still tries to make sure I feel included in social events.

ENCOURAGING EACH OTHER IN OUR CALLINGS

When we both finished seminary, Bill had carved out for himself a ministry at Rider College as chaplain. He did not earn much, but it was sufficient for our needs. I was eager to work, too, but I found it very difficult to find a ministry close enough for me to commute. Three months went by without any leads. Bill would come home from the college and find me depressed and discouraged. When an opportunity came to teach English as a second language in a maximum-security prison for men, he made a great effort to encourage me. "Do you think it is safe?" I asked. "Oh, of course," he said. "I visited some juvenile prisons and they are well guarded. Volunteers are always protected." Thus, I found myself on the first night locked up in a classroom with fifty or so Hispanic murderers, thieves, and illegal numbers racketeers who asked me on the spot to teach them an English lesson. Possibly, the husbands of other women might have been too fearful of encouraging their wives in what looked to be a dangerous situation. But, Bill had more accurate experiential information (on prisons) and love for me that expressed itself in a desire for me to feel satisfied with my life.

My mother had been a phenomenal business entrepreneur. When her brothers did not work with her father in his warehouse business selling and trading scrap metal and burlap sacks, she did it. Together, their business blossomed to the extent that they established connections not only in Puerto Rico, but also in the nearby Dominican Republic. My mother bought property that looked to be nowhere of any importance, but which eventually became the suburb of the city. When she was married, she gave the same zeal to her house. Beautifying her house became her mission in life. But, for me, to spend all my time on a house seemed like a great waste. As we stand at the judgment seat and are asked, "What did you do with the gift of time I gave you?" am I mainly going to say, "I cleaned the house and kept the decoration up to date"? I was afraid that was going to happen to me. But, Bill encouraged me to teach English as a second language. And half a year later, he even helped me obtain my first job in full-time ministry.

While I was teaching in the prison, he was chaplain at Rider College. Another nearby college, Trenton State College (now New Jersey College), was about to lose its chaplaincy. The male chaplain had been discovered to have sexually molested several female college students. The president of the college had been accusing the ministerial board of being too incompetent to hire a qualified, moral chaplain, since this was the second chaplain in a row to succumb to moral failure. So, when my husband heard about this dilemma, he suggested, "Why not now hire a woman?" This was a new idea for all of them, but the school was very enthusiastic. Not only did they hire me, but, when I left, they hired another woman as chaplain. The school felt a female chaplain was safer. By muscling himself into the conversation, Bill was able to get me into paid ministry (and save the ministry as well). I was delighted. I went from Trenton State (prison) to Trenton State (college). Nevertheless, I decided to keep volunteering at the prison with the Spanish Bible study I had begun.

When we were next called to Newark to do a joint ministry, we learned to work together, clarifying each of our roles. After completing seminary, when we worked establishing a college-level center for seminary education (Alpha-Omega Community Theological School [ACTS]), we discovered that, when we both have the same job description, we become inefficient, both doing the same job and becoming insulted because our work has not been accepted by the other as sufficient. Thus, we learned to clarify at the outset what each one is going to do. At that time, he became the director of personnel and I the academic dean. He is gifted in dealing with sticky personnel issues; I enjoy organizing a curriculum. Now, even before we both lead in a worship service, we go over in detail what we are each responsible to do, and then make a point of not meddling in the other's area.

Our relationship was built on dialogue and mutual respect, and this continues today. Even though Bill may not have intuited every possible feeling of oppression or omission I might have sensed, he was always open to conversation. If God is "the One who will be who I will be," Bill had confidence that I could be who God wants me to be.

RESOLVING FAMILIAL ISSUES

So, if I did not feel called to do housework twenty-four hours a day, how could each of us have our joint ministry and yet take care of the daily needs of our house? When we were first married, Bill was limited by ill health. After an intensive urban summer ministry just before we were married, where his supervisor overworked and underpaid him, a potential intestinal disease developed. He was just out of the hospital the day before we were married and recuperating for several months, so I took care temporarily of all the household duties. But, as Bill slowly got better, we began to divide them up. Since I woke up later, Bill prepared breakfast and lunch for us both. I then cooked dinner. Since Bill was allergic to dust, I dusted and vacuumed, while he picked up and cleaned the bathrooms. I did the shopping because I was quicker. Bill eventually washed the clothing in order to balance our household responsibilities when he read that women tend to do more housework than men. Through the years, we have fine-tuned our labor division. What has this done for me? By both of us sharing in making a home, our home belongs to both of us. In addition, from my perspective, it allows me to proclaim God's mighty acts of ministry so that, when I come to God's judgment seat and God asks me what I did with the gift of time, I can answer, "I have tried to love my neighbor—my husband, my family—by making a comfortable home, but also my love has extended outward to the world." We divided our household responsibilities many years before it had become more commonplace, and this, at times, has caused some other Christian men to belittle Bill, as if he were a traitor to his sex. It has not always been pleasant for him (from the outside). But, as a result, we have formed ourselves into a well engaged ministry team.[3]

Calmly discussing how to handle all our differences came to a screeching stop when we had our child. An infant is a twenty-four hour burden that necessitates at least three adults, but we were no longer in the Dominican Republic where a nanny could be hired reasonably, nor were we near family who could help. We discovered that we had differ-

3. For further details, see Spencer et al., *Marriage at the Crossroads,* and Spencer, *Beyond the Curse,* 138–79.

ent philosophies of childrearing. Bill, who lost his sister when he was five from others' negligence at a pool site, was more diligent to establish physical limitations for Steve. And, I, who had been protected from such calamities, was at times more flexible. "He shouldn't jump on the couch!" "Let him jump!" "Let's play with our son." "Let's teach him." We could not always come to agreement. Long-term decisions always have to be made by mutual agreement. But, in the short term, we divided each day up. Bill was responsible from when we first woke up until his mandatory midafternoon siesta. I was responsible for our son from 3:00 P.M. until bedtime. Whoever woke up was responsible during the night. We had to work at allowing the other person to be the one ultimately responsible in quick moments of decision making. Sometimes, people ask us, who is the final decision maker? The answer is, we take turns—by time and by gifting. It has worked well. I was able to complete my Ph.D. during these years. Our son was born one September at the beginning of my studies. I took the fall semester off. In the spring, I studied every morning and Bill worked at night teaching adult literacy. I had to be focused. I did not waste any time Monday through Thursday mornings. And, I ended up finishing my studies in three and a half years! Bill helped make that possible by sharing in childcare as well as household duties. Since, at the doctoral level, I only had three classes to attend each semester, I could have more time for study than at the master's level. I had confidence in Bill's childcare, and he was able to give plenty of attention to our son.

DEALING WITH CHALLENGES IN WORK

Every stage in our life brought new challenges. We had planned to trade off ministry opportunities. Bill had the first ministry opportunity as a chaplain at Rider College. We both were called to the second ministry opportunity as Bible teachers with New York Theological Seminary. I then had the third ministry opportunity to teach at Gordon-Conwell Theological Seminary, and Bill then had to find his calling here. It was not easy for him. He wanted to write, but he also wanted something more. Finally, after a year of looking, he was invited to teach theology in summer school at Gordon-Conwell. He then decided to obtain his doctorate at Boston University. Now, he teaches half-time at Gordon-Conwell's Boston campus, while I teach full time at the Hamilton campus.

Probably one of the most difficult challenges in our marriage revolved around our desk. Thinking to be good stewards, I thought we could share a desk at home. Bill could use the desk in the morning, and I would use it in the afternoon. Although I had an office at school, I preferred to prepare my lectures at home so I could concentrate better and be around my family. All we had to do was pick up our papers at the end of our time period so it could be used by the next person. Bill, however, now felt oppressed by me. He saw the situation from a different perspective. He was supposed to be a writer, but he did not have his own space. He wanted his own office at home. But, what could we do, since our home was small and we had no money to buy a new house? After many months of vigorous discussions, we thought we would try buying another desk to see if that would help. We bought a wooden desk sold by our colleague Roger Nicole. Our office now had two desks. When we could afford it, we had a skylight installed for more light right over Bill's desk. And, to our surprise, that was enough. We did not need separate rooms. Bill was happy to have his own space. I was happy we could afford this new arrangement. Thus, I needed to remember that, even as Bill had encouraged me in my ministry so I could do all I thought God wanted me to do, I too had to make sure that Bill could do all he thought God wanted him to do. Through the years, we had been working to become interdependent. But, two independent people who are becoming one flesh are still two individuals. We also needed our own space, our own turf, even as we shared one space.

When we marry, we marry for "sickness and in health." When we were first married, I tried to create a healing environment for my husband. In 2004, I, who considered myself the healthy one, who ate well and exercised regularly, was found to have breast cancer. If there was one illness I did not want, it was breast cancer. Cancer seemed to me such a terrifying illness, since at the end it appeared to be so painful. In addition, it was embarrassing! What woman wants to explain that her breast is sick! What Bill did for me is help me look straight at what I had and search for the very best care we could find. We decided not to undergo surgery at our local hospital, but instead to travel about an hour to Massachusetts General Hospital, which had a center specializing in breast cancer—the surgeons only did breast surgery, and the team of doctors only dealt with breast cancer. Together with our co-pastor, Leslie McKinney, we researched the best place to go. I discovered I had breast cancer just before I had to go on an overnight speaking engagement. While I was gone, Bill and Leslie called every Boston hospital to find the best surgeon. After the removal of the cancer, Bill took seriously his care of me and never treated me as an inferior person. In addition, despite inconvenience to himself, since he was teaching intensive courses, he came with me on once-a-month travels to distant beach sites so I could enjoy physically and mentally the healing salt water. He brought me to these good lands, even as God, the healer, brought the Israelites to Canaan.

PLANNING FOR MATURE DEVELOPMENT

We spent many years cooperating together to become one flesh. Now, I find we are also working on our unique callings. At age sixty, I decided to lower my course load by one in order to have a more pleasant fall curricular experience. Since it took Bill longer to establish his half-time teaching schedule, he has no idea yet when he will lessen his load. He teaches four courses, while I teach six. If we ever find a new ministry opportunity, we would want it to be one where we both are happy. Our God is "I will be who I will be." What is the future? We do not know, but we do know that our God is the hope for the future, our God is always acting, our God is a mystery, but God is also always near, and God is sovereign. We want to serve God together as our bodies allow, for as long as God empowers us. As we age, we want slowly to increase our rest and decrease our work, but never stop serving the Lord.

SUMMARY

How, then, did Bill help me become the person God intended? Part of the answer was who Bill was, who he saw me to be, and a host of means. Bill is motivated by love, is willing to change, accepts my weaknesses and strengths, faces the truth, and courageously endures the cost of his convictions. He sees me as a person whom God has gifted for ministry; thus, he encourages me to think and to envision and to act. Some of the means by which we lived were dialogue, mutual respect and confidence, encouragement by words and deeds, willingness to discuss misunderstandings, division of labor by gifts, active promotion, sharing in small things (such as household duties and child care) so larger goals could be accomplished, readiness to handle challenges as they happen, and remembering that encouragement goes two ways. A small incident can make a big difference. The abstract necessitates the specific. But, most important of all is to rely on God's sovereign care.

10

Conclusion

KeumJu Jewel Hyun
and
Cynthia Davis Lathrop

THE AUTHORS OF THE preceding chapters have shown us how women can blossom to their fullness in Christ when godly men are behind them.

Today, we hear many painful stories about abusive men: controlling fathers keeping their daughters from becoming who they can be, insecure husbands being jealous of their wives' success in their careers, or indoctrinated pastors keeping women from exercising their God-given gifts to their full potential. Contrary to such men, here, we meet the men who are strong in their self-identity, upright in their character, and loving in their hearts. Among these men, we see many common threads and shared characteristics.

Some men came alongside the women in their lives coaching and teaching; some encouraged them to pursue further studies. Some men took a supportive role, helping to advance women responding to their respective callings. They were sensitive to the hopes and fears that the women had and became advocates as well as role models. They were patient and selfless—one husband even took retirement from his rewarding job to help his wife to take on a new career. Looking ahead to the future, they shared their lives and experiences and prepared the women to become effective to serve in their respective areas of calling.

Husbands took their wives as equal partners. They honored their wives' wishes; they were attentive to and inclined their ears to the worthy things their wives had to say. Although no man was mentioned as an egalitarian per se, each man seemed to believe in biblical equality, and none of them opposed women's leadership in the church; in fact, one pastor even defended a woman teaching an adult Sunday school class. They simply carried out the roles God had given them—father, husband, brother, pastor, colleague, ministry worker, or businessman; their attitude toward the women was that of Christ—to obey God the Father in heaven (cf. Phil 2:5ff).

The fathers carried out the parental role that God gave to them. They loved and brought their daughters up with the "discipline and instruction approved by the Lord" (Eph 6:4 NLT). They guided and helped their daughters to choose the way God wanted them to go (cf. Prov 22:6) and took the father's responsibility of teaching their daughters to be deeply rooted in the word of God. They kept their daughters' inquisitiveness alive by taking the time to explain things when their daughters asked questions; they did not dismiss their questions as insignificant.

These men truly helped their wives, daughters, or parishioners to become the kind of persons whom God wanted them to be. Thus, they were God's stewards who helped these women to grow in Christ and become more like him. All of them were countercultural, just as Jesus was when he was on earth. Against cultural mandate, they sent their daughters to school when the norm was to send only boys to school. Some men saw the gifts the women possessed and recognized the potential of what they could be for God; thus, they gave the women opportunities to fully develop their gifts. In addition, the men were able to see the women as individuals created in God's image rather than only in how they related to men.

Through the stories, these men remind us that:

- God created male and female in his image for his glory and commanded both man and woman to be good stewards of his creation (Gen 1:26–28).

- Woman and man are fearfully and wonderfully made (Ps 139:13–14) and are God's workmanship (Eph 2:10).

- God has a purpose for women when he brings them into the world (Jer 1:5).

- Husbands are commanded to love their own wives and not to be harsh with them (Eph 5:28, Col 3:18) and to give honor to their wives and treat them with understanding (1 Pet 3:7).

- We women are equally responsible for helping our husbands to become the persons whom God created them to be.

The men mentioned in this book supported the women wholeheartedly. These men demonstrated their responsibility as God's coworkers to help women to become effective as God's workers.

Now what do these stories of supportive men have to do with the rest of us? It is a matter of honoring God's creation mandate. By the grace of God's favor, the men mentioned in this book brought honor to God by being the support behind their beloved women. Thus, men and women together bring glory to God as they walk in the original intent of the Lord.

May the Lord bestow his favor upon you!

Afterword

John P. Lathrop

IN 1865, A POEM by William Ross Wallace was published, entitled "The Hand that Rocks the Cradle." This poem spoke of the power that women, specifically mothers, have in influencing their children. Though the poem does not go into the specifics of how women impact the lives of children, experience would tell us that mothers influence them by their words and their ways, by the things that they say and the things that they do. In other words, they influence the young by how they relate to them. The sphere of influence that the poem refers to is the domestic sphere, the home. That is one place in which a woman can have influence and excel, but it is certainly not the only place. This book demonstrates that women make a difference outside of the home as well; they have influence in areas such as business, education, and Christian ministry.

The ability to influence is not limited to women. By the stories you have read, the authors have shared with us a piece of their lives (1 Thess 2:8). Men played a tremendous, critical role to influence and shape the lives of these women. The writers have shared stories of the help and encouragement that they have received from key men in their lives. Along life's journey, each of the writers has encountered men who encouraged, ministered, and urged them to live lives worthy of God (1 Thess 2:11–12). These men have selflessly made choices that moved the women they know into places of ministry where they could grow in confidence and gifting, advancing God's kingdom inside and outside church walls.

Those men who encouraged and supported the authors of this book are a father, brother, husband, pastor, or other Christian man who has contributed to building these women into the persons that they are today. Some of the men have been family members, and others have come from outside the family. In some cases, the men who supported the women were of a different cultural and ethnic background from the women whom they encouraged. All of this seems to show us that there is not just one specific group of men who could encourage women.

Every day, we are sending messages, and every day they are being read, whether we are conscious of it or not. Those men whom we have read about in this book have sent a message in a variety of ways. They were approachable; they have been open to and have communicated with these women by taking, or making, time for them. Their encouragement extended beyond giving time; it had other aspects as well. Some supported by spoken words, others by assuming certain duties so that the woman could pursue her goals and develop her gifts. They also showed confidence in these women and provided them with opportunities that they might grow into their full potential.

Let me speak to the men here. We are all communicating every day. We communicate by words and actions. Then the question is, "What are we communicating?" Specifically, what are we communicating to the women in our lives: to our daughters, our wife, the women in our church, or our coworkers? What are they "hearing" from us? Do they feel valued and affirmed or unimportant and left out? Perhaps we have never really thought about it. It is time to start thinking about it. Reading this book can be very convicting. If you have found that you should have been better in encouraging and supporting, don't despair. This realization may be the wake-up call that helps you to change. This book contains a wealth of examples of things that you can practically do to become a "hero." You will, of course, have to adapt the principles to your own situation, but you are not alone. There are those who have trod the path that you desire to walk on. We have the expressed statements of Scripture and the examples contained in this book. Sometimes, we need to see the principles of Scripture fleshed out in the life of another in order for us to better understand what to do. In this book, we find models to follow.

Taking the time and effort to encourage and support women is something worth pursuing. It is worthwhile, first, because it will help us men be more of what God desires us to be. We, like Paul, are to encourage both men and women (1 Thess 2:12). It is also a worthwhile endeavor because it can bear some amazing fruit. We can be coworkers with God in helping foster women of influence. You could right now have a wife or daughter who has great potential to impact the world and advance

God's kingdom. You may be an employer who works with women who could excel in your company. You may be a pastor who has a woman or women in your congregation with great gifting and promise. Some of these women may reach their full stature and use and develop all of their gifts on their own. Some, however, may not do so unless they are encouraged or given opportunity. Let us purpose to acknowledge their gifts and talents and advocate for them to continue to become all that they can be. Let us provide opportunities for them to use their God-given gifts so that they may reach their full potential for the glory of God.

Contributors

Gwendolyn Joy Dewey has a doctorate from the University of Washington in educational policy, governance, and administration, and a Doctor of Ministry from Eastern Baptist Theological Seminary in transformational leadership for the global church. She is the Bakke Graduate University Academic Dean over both the School of Theology and the School of Business, the Director of Doctoral Dissertations, and Administrator of the Theology of Work grant program. She was past President of Bakke Graduate University and teaches in the U.S. and globally. She has experience both in the corporate world and in education (pre-kindergarten through university levels), holding key administrative positions at each level. She served as professor in the graduate educational administration program at Pacific Lutheran University, Tacoma, Washington.

Nancy Hudson is an American missionary to South Africa since 1989. She planted and built ten churches, starting the pioneer work under a mango tree with five people. She also trained pastors, teachers, and leaders in the ministry through Christian Assemblies of South Africa. Originally from New Brighton, Pennsylvania, Nancy was commissioned by her home church, Christian Assembly of New Brighton under the International Fellowship of Christian Assemblies. Nancy has three grown children and eight grandchildren.

KeumJu Jewel Hyun is founder and President of Matthew 28 Ministries, Inc., a nonprofit organization that seeks to train pastors and church leaders and to develop Christian women's leadership in Kenya. She is an adjunct professor of Bakke Graduate University, Seattle, a longtime Bible teacher, and a lecturer. Jewel holds Master of Arts in New Testament and Doctor of Ministry degrees from Gordon-Conwell Theological Seminary, South Hamilton, Massachusetts, and a Master of Science degree in Nuclear Physics from Yonsei University, Seoul, Korea. Prior to her studies at the seminary, she worked for more than twenty-five years in the field of information technology in the financial industry and had her own consulting company. Jewel and her husband have two grown children and four grandchildren, and reside in North Billerica, Massachusetts.

Médine Moussounga Keener has a Ph.D. from the University of Paris 7 Jussieu (Now called Université Paris Diderot), where she wrote a dissertation in African American women's history. She teaches French at Eastern University. She was a war refugee in her home country of the Republic of Congo. Médine is married to New Testament scholar Craig Keener. Together, they wrote a booklet on ethnic reconciliation for use in Africa.

Cynthia Davis Lathrop attended Western Connecticut State University and Gordon-Conwell Theological Seminary. She served as one of the copy editors of the book *Apostles, Prophets, Evangelists, Pastors, and Teachers Then and Now* (Xulon Press, 2008). Cynthia is a deacon at the Christian Pentecostal Church of Newton and has participated in ministry overseas in Kenya and Indonesia. She is married to John Lathrop, and they have five adult children and three grandchildren.

John P. Lathrop is a graduate of Western Connecticut State University, Zion Bible College, and Gordon-Conwell Theological Seminary. He is an ordained minister with the International Fellowship of Christian Assemblies and has been involved in pastoral ministry for twenty years. He has contributed to *Priscilla Papers*, a publication of Christians for Biblical Equality; *Vista Magazine*, the official publication of the International Fellowship of Christian Assemblies; and *The Pneuma Review*, a publication of the Pneuma Foundation. He wrote two chapters for the book *The Foundations of Faith: Our Beliefs About God and His Works*, edited by Nicholas Cacciatore (Winepress Publishing, 2007) and has one book of his own: *Apostles, Prophets, Evangelists, Pastors, and Teachers Then and Now* (Xulon Press, 2008). John has ministered in Indonesia and Zimbabwe. He is married to Cynthia Lathrop.

Dr. Alice P. Mathews most recently served as Academic Dean of the Gordon-Conwell Theological Seminary, where she had previously co-directed the Doctor of Ministry program and taught in the classroom. Prior to the past thirty years in theological education, she and her husband, Randall, served United States churches and overseas missions in Europe for three decades. They have four grown children and six splendid grown grandsons.

Contributors

Judy W. Mbugua, an ordained pastor, is founder and National Chairperson of Homecare Spiritual Fellowship. She is currently serving as the Continental Coordinator of the Pan African Christian Women Alliance, a commission of the Association of Evangelicals in Africa. She is also the International Chairperson for Women of Global Action. Judy is a lecturer at Haggai Institute for Advanced Leadership; author of several books and chapters including her autobiography, *Judy: A Second Chance;* the editor of *Women as Risk Takers;* and a sought-after speaker. Judy holds two honorary degrees: a Doctor of Theology from Latin University of Theology, U.S.A., and a Doctor of Ministry degree from the European Theological Seminary, Birmingham, U.K. She is a mother of five children and grandmother of ten.

Aída Besançon Spencer is Professor of New Testament at Gordon-Conwell Theological Seminary. She has served as a community organizer for Community Action–Plainfield, instructor of English as a second language, college chaplain at Trenton State College, Adjunct Professor at New York Theological Seminary, master in residence for Alaythia House of The Salvation Army, and Academic Dean for Alpha-Omega Community Theological School. She has also published thirteen books and one hundred and seven other chapters, articles, and book reviews (as of 2009). She is married to William David Spencer. Both are ordained ministers of the word and sacrament with the Presbyterian Church U.S.A. Their adult son Stephen, a chef for nine years and a musician, is currently studying communication and media production.

William David Spencer is co-author most recently of *Marriage at the Crossroads: Couples in Conversation about Discipleship, Gender Roles, Decision Making and Intimacy* (IVP: 2009). He is Ranked Adjunct Associate Professor of Theology and the Arts at Gordon-Conwell Theological Seminary, Pastor of Encouragement with Pilgrim Church, (Beverly, Massachusetts), Editor of *Priscilla Papers,* and the author of ten books and one hundred fifty-seven chapters, articles, poems, stories, editorials, and book reviews. He is married to Aída Besançon Spencer.

Elke Werner is the founder and Director of Women in God's Service (WINGS), based in Germany. She has a heart for evangelism and justice and is involved in mentoring younger women leaders. Elke serves as Senior Associate for Women in Evangelism in the International Lausanne

Movement, is on the board of Lausanne International, and has been active in helping shape the Third Lausanne Congress in Capetown. She is also on the board of World Vision Germany and part of the Leighton Ford Mentoring Community. She has authored more than ten books in German and is in high demand as a speaker and teacher at women's conferences both in Germany and other European countries. Born in Duisburg, Germany, Elke resides with her husband, Dr. Roland Werner, in Marburg, a quaint medieval university town in the middle of Germany. Together they lead an interdenominational community church, Christus-Treff, which works within the framework of the German Lutheran Church.

Appendix

From Locker Room to Meeting Room: Restructuring
Groups for Both Women and Men

William David Spencer

N o matter how secure the veneer of civilization has been electro-plated on us men, sometimes when we got into groups a kind of pack psychology takes over. Since most groups have the option of becoming either community or mob, our male vision usually opts either for (1) a hierarchy (somebody calling all the shots) or (2) a group of specialists with a coordinator (who encourages different members to call different shots).

Most of us men have been trained to talk easily, quickly, and assertively. We tend to plunge in and verbally hack away at a problem until it appears solved. Then later somebody patches up the holes.

Many women, I've noticed, tend to discuss before acting, especially in formal group settings. At one planning workshop, we were assigned to meet in a classroom. "I guess we ought to form a circle," one woman said. I grabbed a chair and began dragging it across the floor when I discovered I was alone. The women were still back at the rows of chairs deciding how best to move them to least disrupt the present arrangement. This was true efficiency: how to get maximum accomplishment for a minimum of physical effort.

Many men may feel more comfortable working out ahead of time what we want to accomplish or to present in a group. We don't like to change our basic stance while a group is actually meeting. We'll think about new issues afterwards, but, if we have selected a goal, we'll go for it relentlessly. Many men like to make real decisions in the offices beforehand. We come to meetings to rubberstamp those decisions and to gossip generally in the remaining time.

Women, understandably, do not feel comfortable hanging around in the locker-room camaraderie of male offices. Instead, they come to meetings to hash out issues, to come to decisions, and to build relationships. If my wife gets new information in the middle of a meeting, she wants to think about it immediately and may change her position because of it. Many women are frustrated with men's "quick closure" and apparently "hasty decisions."

Additionally, while not all women may be polite, most women have been trained to be polite, so they often feel guilty about interrupting. This is seldom a U.S. male problem. As a result, many times, women don't get an opening for their ideas until the decision has been made. The men get impatient at their late responses, or worse, laugh at women's responses as inappropriate.

What can be done? Men who want groups structured for everyone's participation need to make sure either that group decisions are reached by the whole group *at the meeting,* or that women are invited to participate in the office bull sessions.

When groups meet, statements that cut off or ridicule others should be dropped. If we shut up some of the time, women will find the space to speak. If we don't always jump in with the first response or if we limit our responses, a byproduct will be fewer un-thought-out and—let's face it—stupid responses as well.

Soliciting responses from women is good if it's not done in either a gruesome, challenging manner or with a patronizing attitude. Try, "I'd like to hear what Jane has to say about this." "Sure," says Jane, shocked, then expanding after a moment's pause, "I think. . . ." Body motion can help here, too. Turning toward Jane and looking interested invites her response and effectively blocks off Ralph, the chronic dominator.

Once a woman speaks, we ought to give positive feedback—even if we disagree. And think about her point. Maybe she's right. She'll think about your point and maybe switch over. Ralph, on the other hand, probably won't think about either of your points. You may switch to her side, she may switch to yours, but at least you'll see two sides of the issue.

Repeating a woman's idea to ensure that it has been heard may sometimes be necessary. And, when it is adopted, everyone needs to know that it was Jane's idea, that it just didn't come out of the air. Giving credit where it's due may help the Ralphs look toward the Janes for future insights.

We should also accord women their fair share of leadership. Supporting women's leadership will make the group more effective and egalitarian.

Many of our working lives—secular and sacred—are spent in meetings small and large. Even worship services are mainly sacred meetings, with a couple of "holy" people monopolizing them. Heaven is bringing in a new order, where every captive is released, every believer made heir. We might as well structure that kind of participation here on earth. It'll enrich our community, serve women, and ease the eventual shock.

In summary, what do we men need to do to support women in groups? Make sure women are included in the actual decision making. Make a space for women's responses; limit our responses. Invite women's responses in a nonthreatening manner. Support those responses with at least a grunt of gratitude. Never ridicule women's responses; don't cut them off. Help block off dominators who would keep women silent. Repeat women's ideas and opinions if necessary. Give full credit for ideas to the women who make them. Make certain women are afforded their full, equal share of leadership. Consciously support women when they are leaders. This process will enrich any group while stealing nothing from men's full share. Best of all, it will please God, who created female and male together to express God's image.

Reprinted from *Daughters of Sarah* 13:3
(May/June 1987): 22–23.

Bibliography

Bakke, Dennis. *Joy at Work: A Revolutionary Approach to Fun on the Job.* Seattle: PVG, 2005.

Kauffman, Richard A. "Apostle to the City, Part 2." *Christianity Today,* March 3, 1997. Online: http://www.christianitytoday.com/ct/1997/march3/7t336b.html.

McKenna, David. *Power to Follow, Grace to Lead.* Nashville: W Publishing Group, 1989.

———. *Never Blink in a Hailstorm and Other Lessons on Leadership.* Grand Rapids: Baker, 2005.

Moussounga, Jacques. *Biographie de Papa Jacques.* Unpublished.

Smith, Brad, William Hendricks, and Raymond Bakke. *Joy at Work Bible Study Companion.* Seattle: PVG, 2005.

Smith, James Bryan. *The Good and Beautiful God: Falling in Love With the God Jesus Knows.* Downers Grove, Ill.: InterVarsity, 2009.

Spencer, Aída Besançon. *Beyond the Curse: Women Called to Ministry.* Peabody, Mass.: Hendrickson, 1985.

Spencer, William David, Aida Bensançon Spencer, Steven R. Tracy, and Celestia G. Tracy. *Marriage at the Crossroads: Couples in Conversation about Discipleship, Gender Roles, Decision Making and Intimacy.* Downers Grove, Ill: InterVarsity, 2009.

Wallace, William Ross. "The Hand that Rocks the Cradle." Online: http://en.wikipedia.org /wiki/The_Hand_That_Rocks_the_Cradle_(poem).

Witherington, Ben III. *Women in the Ministry of Jesus.* Cambridge: University Press, 1987.